TALES *from the* DUGOUT

TALES *from the* DUGOUT

The Greatest True
Baseball Stories Ever Told

MIKE SHANNON

CONTEMPORARY BOOKS

Library of Congress Cataloging-in-Publication Data

Shannon, Mike.
    Tales from the dugout : the greatest true baseball
stories ever told / Mike Shannon.
        p.   cm.
    Includes index.
    ISBN 0-8092-3107-7 (hardcover)
    ISBN 0-8092-2950-1 (paperback)
    1. Baseball—Anecdotes.   I. Title.
GV873.S45   1997
796.357—dc21   97-223
                                                   CIP

Cover illustration copyright © Todd L. W. Doney
Illustrations by Don Pollard

Published by Contemporary Books
A division of NTC/Contemporary Publishing Group, Inc.
4255 West Touhy Avenue, Lincolnwood (Chicago), Illinois 60712-1975 U.S.A.
Copyright © 1997 by Mike Shannon
Printed in the United States of America
International Standard Book Number: 0-8092-3107-7 (hardcover)
                                                   0-8092-2950-1 (paperback)
  01   02   03   04   LB   22   21   20   19   18   17   16   15   14   13   12   11   10   9   8   7

CONTENTS

PREFACE

OK, let's get one thing out of the way right now: I'm not the ex–St. Louis Cardinals outfielder–third baseman. I'm the "other" Mike Shannon. Not that I mind your asking. For one thing, you bought this book, so . . . "I love you, man!" For another, it shows that you were paying attention to baseball back in the sixties when Mike and the rest of the Cards went to three World Series.

And I can understand why you might be momentarily confused. After all, the "other Mike Shannon" (from my perspective) has been a member of the baseball media for a good while now—Mike joined the Cardinals' broadcast booth after he retired as a player—and he even lent his name to a baseball newsletter that was on the scene for a brief time. On the other side of the coin, someday somebody is going to watch me play fast-pitch softball and say, "Hey, Mike Shannon, didn't you used to play third base for the St. Louis Cardinals?" It could happen!

Actually, Mike and I go way back. When I was a Little Leaguer in Jacksonville, Florida, Mike played one summer for our Triple A Jacksonville Suns on his way up to the Show. That right there made Mike my *second*-favorite player (as cool as it was to have the same name as a major leaguer, I wasn't about to ditch Willie Mays for anybody). Then, at Bishop Kenny High School, a classmate, who knew absolutely nothing about baseball, nicknamed me "Moonman." Wow! The same moniker as Mike. Unfortunately, I couldn't get the nickname to stick. I guess I just didn't do or say as many flaky things as Mike. For instance, Bob Gibson tells a "Moonman" story in *A Stranger to the Game* about the third game of the 1964 World Series. On the first pitch of the bottom of the ninth inning, Mickey Mantle hit a gargantuan home run off Barney Schultz into the third deck of Yankee Stadium to win the game 2–1. Gibson remembers watching the soaring home run and seeing the Cardinals' rightfielder, Shannon, "poised with one leg on the fence as if he were going to jump up and catch the damn thing." Afterward, when Gibson asked him if he really thought he might be able to catch the ball, Shannon said, "You never know, Big Boy. You never know."

I did eventually meet the other Mike Shannon. In fact, I interviewed him. It was after I had moved to Cincinnati and started publishing *Spitball: The Literary Baseball Magazine*. We were doing a special retrospective on Roger Maris in commemoration of the 25th anniversary of his great, record-breaking 61-home-run season of 1961, and I wanted to talk to Shannon about Maris because the two of them had become close friends after Maris was traded from the Yankees to the Cardinals. I caught up with Shannon at Riverfront Stadium during batting practice before a game between the Cardinals and the hometown Reds. Introducing myself only as the editor of *Spitball*, I asked Mike if he'd talk to me about Roger Maris for our special issue. Mike agreed to talk but asked me to catch him later in the press-box dining room after he himself finished conducting some interviews for the Cards' radio show that evening.

I didn't mention my name in the press-box dining room either. I wanted to act like a professional writer, not a fan. I didn't think I was nervous, but I must have been. While Shannon ate his dinner (nothing but a bowl of salad), I began the interview, asking, "When he first came over from the Yankees, did Mike have any trouble fitting in with the Cardinals?"

Shannon looked up from his salad and said, "You mean 'Roger'?"

"Uh, yeah . . . right, 'Roger,'" I blurted in consternation at the mix-up. Shannon went into a lengthy answer, and I listened intently while I studied his face—so this is what Mike Shannon looks like and sounds like—and mentally formulated my next question. And then I did it again.

"How instrumental was Mike to the team's success in 1967 and 1968?" I asked.

"You mean 'Roger'?" said Shannon again.

"Yes, I mean 'Roger.'" Boy, he must think I'm goofy, I thought in exasperation.

Thankfully I got through the rest of the interview, which turned out to be pretty darn good, without referring to Roger Maris as "Mike," and Shannon kindly never questioned me about my Freudian slips. From one "Moonman" to another: thanks, Mike.

A few years later my baseball name caused somebody else some confusion, yet that person also spared me any embarrassment. I was working on a juvenile biography of Johnny Bench, and I wanted to talk to former Cincinnati Reds manager Sparky Anderson, who had been Bench's manager for most of the great catcher's career.

At the time, Anderson was managing the Detroit Tigers. I called the Tigers' offices, the operator switched me promptly to the clubhouse, and to my surprise Sparky almost immediately came on the line.

"Sparky, this is Mike Shannon and—" I got no further than that.

"Mike! How ya doing? It's good to hear from you. How's the ball club doing?" When he had been with Cincinnati in the National League, Sparky had gotten to know that "other" Mike Shannon as an opposing player and later as a Cardinals broadcaster.

"Sparky," I said soberly, "I'm not *that* Mike Shannon. I'm a writer in Cincinnati."

"Oh. Well, what can I do for you, Mike?" Sparky asked. I told him what I was up to, and then he proceeded to patiently answer all my questions, fully and graciously and without the least hint of irritation, demonstrating to me that the reality of Sparky Anderson matches the image of Sparky Anderson as one of the nicest people you will ever meet in baseball.

When I started working on this book, I realized that the idea of a book of baseball anecdotes was nothing new; however, since the typical baseball anecdote book has always repeated many of the same old stories, my goal was to write a book full of *new* anecdotes. Since baseball books have appeared in the last decade and a half with the frequency of home runs at Coors Field, I wanted the serious, as well as the casual, baseball-book buyer to have a good reason to purchase this book. That reason is the fact that, with very few exceptions, the stories in this book have never appeared in any other baseball book. I hope you are entertained by the book; I feel confident you won't find it to be, as Yogi Berra would put it, "déjà vu all over again."

There is nothing more fun in writing a book like this than meeting and talking to the people who supply many of the stories herein. The morning I spent at the home of Herman "Flea" Clifton is typical of the experience, in that you never know when and where you'll find a good story. Mr. Clifton was born in Cincinnati in 1909, but he grew up idolizing and modeling himself after the great Ty Cobb. Mr. Clifton realized his dream of playing for the Detroit Tigers, but he had the misfortune of being a natural second baseman at the same time that another Tiger named Charlie Gehringer was in his prime. Although he was never a regular in his four major league seasons, Mr. Clifton spent about three hours of his precious time telling me his personal baseball story. Several times during our session Mr. Clifton said, "I hope I'm telling you something that will be useful for your book." Although I assured him that he was being most helpful, the truth was that we concluded our interview without his having said anything I could work into an interesting story. I packed up my tape recorder, notebook, pens, and *Baseball Encyclopedia*; sincerely thanked him for his time; and started to walk out of the small kitchen where we had talked. "You know, I remember something else," he said. He said this offhandedly, not knowing he was about to finally give me what I'd come for, but that's exactly what it turned out to be: a wonderful little baseball anecdote that came home in the bottom of the ninth.

In addition to Mr. Clifton, I would like to acknowledge the following persons and publications for their help in compiling some of the stories in this book: Charles Alexander, Marty Appel, *Baseball America*, *Baseball Bulletin*, *Baseball Digest*, *Baseball Weekly*, *Beckett Baseball Card Monthly*, *Bill Mazeroski Baseball*, Tom Boswell, Bobby Bragan, Marty Brennaman, Bob Brigham, Nick Cafardo, *The Chadwick Report*, Eliot Cohen, Jerry Coleman, Robert Connolly, Jim Crowley, John Curtis, Ken Daley, Rick Dempsey, Glenn Dickey, *The Diamond Angle*, *Dodgers Dugout*, Tom Eckel, Charles Einstein, John Erardi, Charley Feeney, Dave Fendrick, Tom Flaherty, *The Flatbush Faithful*, Foxy Gagnon, Peter Gammons, Joe Gergen, Joe Goddard, Wild Bill Hagy, Charles Henderson, Tot Holmes, *Inside Sports*, Stan Isle, Tom Jackson, Jack Jadick, Lloyd Johnson, Cliff Kachline, Roger Kahn, Paul Kaplan, Charles Kaufman, Tyler Kepner, Dave Kindred, Peter Korn, Tom Kramer, Norman E. Kurland, Ken Levine, Michael Lloyd, Rich Marazzi, Len Matuszek, Michael J. McCarthy, Hal McCoy, Joe McGuff, Dick Miller, David Moriah, Edgar Munzel, David Nevard, Dan Neville, *The*

National, T. S. O'Connell, *Oldtyme Baseball News*, Greg Park, David Pietrusza, Bob Ponichtera, Dan Quisenberry, Frank Rashid, *A Red Sox Journal*, *Reds Report*, Jim Reeves, Greg Rhodes, Glenn Sample, SCD, Gary Schatz, Mark Schmetzer, Mark Schraf, Jimmy Smith, *The Sporting News*, Alan Steinberg, Kit Stier, *Sweet Spot*, *Tuff Stuff*, Gordon Verrell, the *Wall Street Journal*, Jon Warden, David Whitford, and Phil Wood. *The Baseball Encyclopedia*, *The Ballplayers*, and *The Dickson Baseball Dictionary* were also extremely helpful for spelling and fact-checking purposes.

Special thanks must go to my parents, John and Willie Shannon; to my kids (Meghann, Casey, Mickey, Babe, and Nolan Ryan); to my All-Star mother-in-law, Mrs. D. (Betty Dermody, as she's known to the rest of the world); to my steadfast friend and supporter Jerry Hazelbaker; to my editor at Contemporary Books, Nancy Crossman, for giving me the hit-away sign; and to her assistant, Alina Cowden, for being around to take my phone calls during rain delays.

Most of all, I thank my beautiful and talented wife, Kathy, who has enriched my life to a magnitude beyond my poor abilities to express. Without her, this book, like most of the good things in my life, would never have been authored.

TALES *from the* DUGOUT

SPARKY ANDERSON

Players and managers have long complained of sportswriters who make up quotes to juice up their stories. If the truth be told, sportswriters haven't been the only ones guilty of fabricating copy.

Tigers manager Sparky Anderson, for one, has been known to stretch the truth like saltwater taffy, as Detroit writer Mike Downey found out at the beginning of the 1984 season.

After the Tigers' fifth straight win to open the season, Downey noticed that Sparky was wearing under his jersey the same Domino's Pizza T-shirt, "The Hot Ones," that he'd been wearing since Opening Day. Downey asked the highly superstitious Anderson if he'd washed the T-shirt yet. Anderson said that he hadn't and that he had no intention of washing the shirt as long as the Tigers' winning streak continued.

After Bret Saberhagen of the Kansas City Royals finally stopped the Tigers in game number 10, Downey offered to supply Sparky with the laundry detergent needed to wash the T-shirt.

"Aw, I just made that stuff up," Anderson said. "I've been washin' the thing all along. Been wearin' it every day, but it's clean."

"Then why'd you let me believe you were going out there smelly every day?" asked the mystified Downey.

"Hey, I got to give the boys from the press somethin' to write about, don't I?" replied Sparky.

AUTOGRAPHS

Robert Connolly of Fort Wayne, Indiana, inherited a very special piece of baseball memorabilia from his father: a baseball signed by the great Babe Ruth. The signature was inevitably somewhat faded but still clearly legible as the Babe's. Most people would have been content to simply enshrine the treasured ball in whichever piece of cabinetry houses the family heirlooms, but the enterprising Connolly had ideas about improving it.

Connolly first attended a minor league game at which Joe DiMaggio was to make a guest appearance. A corps of ushers effectively kept autograph seekers away from DiMaggio, who was watching the game from a box seat, but Connolly smoothly talked his way past them.

"Mr. DiMaggio," Connolly said, "when my father was a boy he got this ball signed by Babe Ruth. I'd be grateful if you would sign it too."

"I'd be honored," said DiMaggio, who took the ball and carefully signed it.

Connolly wanted one more signature on the ball, that of his boyhood hero, Mickey Mantle.

One day during spring training in 1988, Connolly spied Mantle and one of his old cronies sitting around the pool of a Fort Lauderdale hotel. Connolly told Mantle the history of the ball and politely asked him to add his signature to the ball.

"Well, I don't know if I want to be on the same ball as DiMaggio. He was pretty mean to me when I was a rookie, you know," said Mantle, who broke into a big grin when he saw that he'd successfully pulled Connolly's leg. He went ahead and signed.

As Connolly was basking in the satisfaction of having completed his mission to have the signatures of a trio of Yankees demigods on one ball, Mantle's companion, Billy Martin, grabbed the baseball out of Mantle's hand and said, "Here, I'll sign your ball too." Before the startled Connolly could formulate a polite objection, the deed was done, and he was holding a baseball autographed by Ruth, DiMaggio, Mantle, and . . . Martin.

Back home in Indiana, Connolly thoroughly erased the last signature.

Speaking of autographs, on a few occasions a major leaguer has refused to give his John Hancock to a young fan who later became his equal, with interesting results.

One day in the early 1970s the San Francisco Giants played the Chicago Cubs in Wrigley Field. In his haste to board the team bus outside the Giants' clubhouse after the game, San Francisco shortstop Chris Speier brushed past several autograph seekers, including one lanky young Chicagoan named Bill Gullickson, who would soon develop into an outstanding major league pitching prospect.

When Gullickson arrived in the Big Show as a Montreal Expos rookie in 1980, the Expos' regular shortstop was none other than Gullickson's boyhood hero, Chris Speier, who had been obtained from San Francisco early in the 1977 season. Gullickson related the story about being spurned by his hero to his chagrined teammate, and the next day he found a new baseball placed conspicuously in his locker and signed by Chris Speier.

With Tommy Lasorda a similar incident ended quite differently. Lasorda was about 14 years old when New York Giants pitcher Buster Maynard refused to sign for him after a game in Philadelphia. A few years later Maynard found himself in the minors, opposing a young Brooklyn Dodgers farmhand with a long memory named Tommy Lasorda. When Maynard came to bat, Lasorda knocked him down on three consecutive pitches.

As the longtime manager of the Los Angeles Dodgers, Lasorda enjoyed sharing this story with his players. "I always tell my guys to sign autographs," he one said, "or one day that kid could grow up and knock you on your ass."

Sometimes fans don't deserve to receive autographs. When autograph hounds act like jerks, some players just refuse to sign. Others sign but let the recipients know what they think of them.

Cleveland Indians shortstop Mark Lewis was signing baseball cards for a few kids during a spring training workout in 1992 when a grown man pushed the kids aside and demanded that Lewis autograph his Mark Lewis baseball card. Lewis did sign the card but personalized it first: "To a rude man with no manners."

Hall of Fame pitcher Burleigh Grimes also knew how to deal with obnoxious fans. An elderly Grimes was in Cooperstown one summer for Hall of Fame Induction Weekend when

DON
POLLARD

an autograph collector's rudeness rubbed him the wrong way. Grimes signed for the man, then said, "Why don't you take that piece of paper, reach around behind yourself, and shove it up the first opening you find."

When it comes to giving out autographs, there has never been a more accommodating signer than Babe Ruth, especially when the autograph seekers were youngsters. In fact, there is only one recorded instance of the Babe's refusing to sign. That was on the day of Lou Gehrig's funeral.

Former New York Yankees publicity director Red Patterson covered the Gehrig funeral as a sportswriter for the *New York Herald Tribune*, and he remembers what happened when a big car pulled up in front of Christ Episcopal Church in Riverside, New York, and Ruth stepped out. A mob of kids rushed up to the Bambino, asking him for his autograph, but Ruth brushed past them, saying, "I'm sorry, boys and girls. Not today. I'm just here to pay my respects."

BATS

Would baseball be the same grand old game if our favorite players marched up to the plate in a crucial situation toting a "brand X" piece of lumber instead of a Louisville Slugger, an Adirondack Big Stick, or any of the other name-brand bats made by companies such as Worth and Mizuno?

Of course not. Yet that's what major league baseball envisioned when it sent a letter to bat manufacturers that read: "Please be apprised that, effective Nov. 7, 1989, Major League Baseball has advised its clubs to order wooden bats without any manufacturer's identification."

Claiming that the manufacturer's label on the Louisville Slugger used by Rickey Henderson in the 1989 World Series was too big, Major League Baseball was supposedly concerned that the "billboarding" was getting out of hand. More likely, Major League Baseball Properties was trying to soften up the bat companies before springing licensing fees on them.

The bat manufacturers, who accept losses on their major league bat sales in return for exposure, made it clear that they would not stand for the gouging. "No labels, no bats" was their reaction. Happily, baseball rescinded its knot-headed policy, and you can still see your favorite major league player swinging the genuine, clearly labeled article at the ballpark.

In a 10-year career as a backup infielder, Mike Fischlin never came close to making a National or American League All-Star team, but his bat once put in an All-Star Game appearance, at the 1986 Mid-Summer Classic in Houston, Texas, thanks to New York Yankees teammate and American League All-Star first baseman Don Mattingly, who liked the model of bat that Fischlin used.

Mattingly promised not only to use Fischlin's bat, but also to turn the barrel of the bat toward the television camera so that America would be able to read Fischlin's name on it. Fischlin alerted his parents so that they too could catch the proud moment on TV.

As things turned out, Fischlin's bat didn't belong in the All-Star Game any more than Fischlin did, as Mattingly went 0–3 with two strikeouts while wielding Fischlin's starstruck war club.

As a Los Angeles Dodger, Eddie Murray once used a borrowed bat begrudgingly and with completely different results from Mattingly's. About halfway through the 1989 season Murray fell into a little slump at the plate, so Dodgers manager Tommy Lasorda decided, against the workaholic Murray's wishes, to give the slugging first baseman a day off against the Houston Astros in the Astrodome.

Figuring that Murray was too fatigued to get his 36-ounce bat around as quickly as usual, Dodgers infielder Lenny Harris took the lightest bat out of the bat rack (a 32-ouncer) and tried to get Murray to consider using it the next time he batted. "You've been popping the ball up with your heavy bat," said the mischievous Harris, "so here, try this lighter one. This bat will bring you good luck. It's The Chosen One."

"Get out of my face," snarled the brooding Murray, who disdained the mere thought of using such a toothpick of a bat.

Despite the rebuff, Harris bugged Murray about switching bats the rest of the game. In the ninth inning when Lasorda called on him to pinch-hit, Murray took "that little piece of nothing" up to the plate, just to shut Harris up. With two Dodgers on base and Los Angeles trailing 5–4, Murray used The Chosen One to belt a 400-foot home run off Houston's ace reliever, Dave Smith, to give the Dodgers a 7–6 win. Predictably, the effervescent Harris claimed credit for Murray's heroics.

"I guess I owe him a meal at Burger King," said a laughing Murray.

TIM BELCHER

The postgame interview is a routine part of baseball these days, and the questions and answers often seem to follow a script. Occasionally, however, a player will introduce a note of originality into the proceedings. Cincinnati Reds starting pitcher Tim Belcher certainly did after having a bit of a rough time in a game against the San Francisco Giants on the night of June 15, 1993.

The Reds won the game 10–5, but Belcher was relieved with one out in the sixth inning, after having been hit by a Robby Thompson line drive in the third and by a Dave Burba pitch while batting in the bottom of the fifth. After the game reporters flocked to Belcher's locker, only to find that the already-departed pitcher had thoughtfully left them a "cardboard interview" hanging in his cubicle:

"Media members,

"To assist you in your quest for quotes, let us eliminate the needless and often time-consuming volley of intellect while crowding around a cramped cubicle. Please except [*sic*] the following as my 'serious and truthful' account of the game just ended.

"Going after the shot off my shoulder, I wasn't aware that the ball was right beside me or I would have thrown him out! (Fastball, low and away)

"What a nice offensive night for our club. As it turned out, we needed them all.

"Burba gave me a chance to forget about my shoulder during the next inning.

"My spliter [*sic*] was good again tonight.

"Hal Morris can flat hit.

"JR [Reds reliever Jeff Reardon] did a great job.

"Popeye returns."

The last statement refers to the nickname Belcher hung on himself when his forearm swelled up after being hit by a Tony Gwynn line drive about a month earlier, on May 11. "I look like Popeye," said Belcher. "All I need is Olive Oyl and some spinach."

YOGI BERRA

Former Yankees catching great Yogi Berra often swung at pitches out of the strike zone, and more often than not he hit them with unusual authority. This earned him the reputation of being the best bad-ball hitter in baseball. Teammate Bobby Brown, a third baseman who went on to become a doctor and later president of the American League, had a different perspective on it.

"Yogi wasn't really a bad-ball hitter," says Brown. "He just had a bigger strike zone than normal. The height of Yogi's strike zone ran from his eyebrows down to his ankles and from his chest to as far as his arms could reach."

In 1987 the Williamsport Bills of the Double A Eastern League had a catcher named Dave Bresnahan who thought he'd take a play out of Everykid's Neighborhood Playbook. Bresnahan lured the Reading Phillies' Rick Rudblad off third base and into a tag-out at home plate by throwing a peeled potato, not the baseball, into left field on a bogus pickoff attempt. Bresnahan was only trying to have some fun— "I thought it'd be a do-over," he said—but the stunt cost him a $50 fine from the Eastern League and shortly afterward his unconditional release.

Yogi once had his own hot potato to handle.

In the summer of 1985 Berra was in Fargo, North Dakota, to play golf in the Roger Maris Celebrity Cancer Benefit. At some point during the tournament Yogi expressed doubts that North Dakota is one of the nation's leading potato-growing states, as its farmers and publicists claim it to be. "You don't have enough potatoes here to fill my front yard," said Berra.

When the Red River Valley Potato Growers Association got wind of Yogi's remark, they decided to do something to change Yogi's mind and earn some good publicity at the same time. They announced that they were loading an 18-wheel tractor trailer with their potatoes, 23 tons' worth, and heading the truck for Berra's home in Montclair, New Jersey.

When Berra heard this, he gulped, "Boy, I only asked for a bag full." In the end, Yogi did not have to worry about a mountain of spuds blocking his front door, as the Red River

Valley Potato Growers Association arranged to have most of the potatoes donated to a New York charity, Food for Survival. When the tractor trailer pulled out of East Grand Forks, North Dakota, in December, it bore a message about its mission on the side of the trailer: "The Red River Valley & Yogi Go To Bat For The Needy."

The experience hardly made Yogi an expert on the subject. About a year later he was having lunch with an old friend, sportswriter Milton Richman. The waitress asked Yogi if he wanted french fries with his hamburger. Berra said, "Yeah, OK . . . but no potatoes. I'm on a diet."

Kentucky congressman Jim Bunning, who won 100 games and pitched a no-hitter in each major league, has his own Yogi Berra story. "One day when I was with the Detroit Tigers, I was pitching against the Yankees. Bob Turley was coaching first base for the Yankees. The Yankees liked to use Turley there because he was real good at stealing the catcher's signals to the pitcher, and Turley had our signs that day right from the beginning of the game. Turley would whistle when I was going to throw a fastball, and he wouldn't whistle on the curve.

"Hank Bauer was up first. Turley whistled at him, and Bauer lined a hit into left field. Tony Kubek batted next. Turley whistled again, and Kubek hit a line drive right to the second baseman.

"Mickey Mantle was batting third, and I'd had about enough of Turley's shenanigans. I walked over to the first-base coaching box and said to Turley, 'If you whistle to Mantle,

I'm going to drill him with the next pitch.' I then walked halfway to the plate and told Mantle the same thing. My catcher called for a fastball, and Turley whistled. Mantle took that pitch, and with the next pitch I hit Mantle in the leg with a slider.

"Mantle started out to the mound—I think he just wanted to talk things over . . . ha, ha—but the catcher and the umpire jumped out in front of the plate and steered Mickey on down to first.

"Yogi was up next. I started him off with a fastball too, and Turley whistled again. Yogi stepped out of the box, cupped his hands around his mouth, and shouted, 'Jim, he's whistling, but I ain't listening.'"

BIRDS

You've probably been to dozens of baseball games on various levels of play, and you've never seen it happen. But it's not as rare an occurrence as you'd think: the old baseball-bird collision, that is.

It happened, for instance, in 1984, during a July 6 game between the Milwaukee Brewers and the Oakland A's at County Stadium. Batting for the A's, Rickey Henderson hit a routine fly to center, and Brewers centerfielder Rick Manning nonchalantly camped under it. All of a sudden, though, Manning had to run forward and lunge to make the catch. That's because a hawk that had been flying over the field spotted Henderson's fly ball and apparently mistook the baseball for something that it could attack and have for dinner. Instead, the hawk got beaned, diverted the ball, and then fluttered lifelessly onto the outfield grass. A Brewers ball boy removed the dead bird from the field in his baseball glove.

"That was the strangest thing I've ever seen," Manning said afterward. "You could play baseball in a birdcage and never hit the bird."

As for Henderson, he had nothing to feel guilty about, but Brewers fans at the game didn't pass up the opportunity to jeer him.

"When I went back on the field at the end of the inning, the fans were flapping their arms and calling me a killer," he said.

A couple of years later in a 1986 Pacific Coast League game there were Beavers (Portland) and bulls (Tucson Toros) all over the diamond, yet it was a duck that figured in the game's most unusual play.

With two outs in the top of the eighth, Portland had a man (Todd Soares) on second when Randy Day blistered a drive down the left-field line that seemed to be headed for extra-base territory. Out of nowhere a UFD (unidentified flying duck) appeared and collided with the baseball. The unlucky duck dropped onto the turf, and the ball fell right in front of the Tucson leftfielder, Chuck Johnson, who picked the ball up and threw it home to nail Soares, the inning's second "dead duck," trying to score from second.

Portland manager Bill Dancy then approached the home-plate area, but not, as everyone expected, in order to challenge the legality of the way the play turned out. "I've only got one question," said Dancy. "What in the hell is a duck doing in Tucson?"

In the most infamous case of all, Dave Winfield hit a bird during a ball game, but with a throw instead of a batted ball. It happened during a 1983 game when the New York Yankees were visiting Toronto. Winfield in center field and Don Baylor in left were warming up their arms just before the Blue Jays came to bat in the bottom of the third. When it came time to toss the warm-up ball to the ball boy on the left-field foul line, Winfield instead took aim and fired at a seagull sitting on the field about 30 feet inside fair territory.

The ball hit the artificial turf of Exhibition Stadium, bounced up, and caught the seagull squarely, killing it instantly.

Winfield's throw would have made Daniel Boone proud. Not so the Torontonians, who were soon booing in outrage as the ball boy solemnly carried the dead bird off the field wrapped in a white towel. After the game, Winfield was arrested by Toronto police on a charge of cruelty to animals but released after the Blue Jays posted his $500 bail.

The Canadian and New York press had a field day with the incident, but Winfield defused the situation by apologizing and by maintaining that he was merely trying to scare the bird away. Yankees manager Billy Martin concurred that the killing was accidental, telling the press, "He hasn't hit the cutoff man all year." Although Toronto officials cleared Winfield of the charge, baseball fans were slow to let the tempest subside. The Yankees' next road trip took them to Detroit, and during each game of the series Tigers fans flapped their arms and made birdcalls every time Winfield came to bat. Later, the Yankees themselves almost sensationalized the incident. On the cover of a team periodical they featured a group of seagulls hovering around Winfield, but recalled the magazine upon further consideration.

WADE BOGGS

Obnoxious fans have been around as long as the game of professional baseball. Some belligerent, rabbit-eared players are ready to go into the grandstands and attack the loudmouths from the first insult, but smarter players can usually find better ways to respond.

For example, Butch Hobson, the former Red Sox third baseman, was managing in the minors one night when a large group of Marines began giving him and his players hell from the very first pitch of the ball game. Hobson ignored their abuse for several innings but finally decided he'd had enough. In between innings he walked slowly and purposefully over to where four of the most offending Marines were sitting in the front row of the box seats. Once there Hobson asked in a loud and clear voice, "Are you guys double-dating?" That effectively shut up the four Marines, who spent the rest of the night trying to fend off the abuse that was directed at them by the rest of their platoon.

When he was still with the Red Sox, five-time American League batting champion Wade Boggs also used his brain instead of his fists to combat a loudmouth. Every time the Red Sox would go into Yankee Stadium, some box-seat bigmouth would start yelling clever things at Wade such as "Boggs, you suck!" Boggs could never pick the guy out in the stands.

One day Boggs was warming up in front of the Boston dugout, and his tormentor started yelling, "Boggs, you suck!" Wade kept glancing up into the grandstands but couldn't pick the guy out, because he wouldn't yell until the point at which Wade had to concentrate on the ball being thrown back to him. For several throws Wade listened carefully, and soon he had narrowed down the loudmouth's location as much as possible. On the next return throw, Boggs stepped to the side, let the ball pass, and zeroed in on his nemesis when he shouted once again, "Boggs, you suck!"

The loudmouth turned out to be a big fat guy who had a couple of burly friends sitting next to him. Boggs walked directly over to the man and said, "Are you the guy who's always yelling at me?"

The man said, "Yeah, it's me."

Boggs said, "Well, why are you always on my case?"

The man merely shrugged his shoulders.

Boggs took a new baseball out of his back pocket, autographed it, tossed it to the man, and then went on about his business.

The man never yelled obscenities at Boggs again and, in fact, became Boggs's biggest fan at Yankee Stadium.

BOOKS

For his great novel *Shoeless Joe* W. P. Kinsella invented a character named Eddie Scissons, who never played a day of major league baseball in his life but goes around anyway claiming to be "the oldest living Chicago Cub." Kinsella says that he got the idea for this wonderful character from several real-life baseball frauds he had met over the years and that such impostors are invariably dumbfounded to learn that their claims can be disproven with a simple check of *The Baseball Encyclopedia*, the venerated official record book of major league baseball, published since 1969 by the Macmillan Publishing Company.

As useful as it is in tripping up the Eddie Scissonses of the world, *The Baseball Encyclopedia* has not always been infallible. Lou Proctor is one fraud who survived the first five editions of *The Encyclopedia*. From 1969 through the 1982 fifth edition, *The Encyclopedia* listed Proctor as having played one game, in 1912 for the St. Louis Browns, during which he drew a walk in the only plate appearance of his entire career. No information about Proctor's size, batting and throwing preferences, position played, or birth and death was ever uncovered or listed, and with good reason: Lou Proctor was not a major league ballplayer but rather a Western Union teletype operator who inserted his name into a wire service box score of a game between the Browns and the Boston Red Sox, apparently as a prank. The ruse was discovered when a baseball researcher compared the corrupted Lou Proctor box score of the May 17, 1912, game with one from a Boston paper, which was compiled independently of the one sent over the wires by Proctor. The box score from the Boston paper showed that it was not Proctor but Pete Compton, a legitimate six-year major leaguer, who pinch-hit for St. Louis pitcher Jack Powell and drew a walk in the seventh inning of the May 17 game.

It was a nice try, Lou, but your demise demonstrates that there are none more tenacious than the researchers who strive to maintain the purity of the greatest record book in all of sport.

There is no greater oxymoron than "baseball autobiography." Ballplayers don't write autobiographies; they dictate them to the professional A.T.T. (as told to) writers who are the real authors of the books. In fact, ballplayers usually don't even write the forewords and introductions that bear their names. And, in addition to actually doing the writing, one of the primary tasks of the professional writer is making what the player says fit for public consumption.

John Erardi, coauthor of *Cincinnati's Crosley Field: The Illustrated History of a Classic Ballpark*, made this latter point at a CASEY Awards Banquet, at which his book was being honored. At the beginning of his acceptance speech Erardi mentioned the introduction to his book, which was supposedly written by Joe Nuxhall, the ex–Cincinnati Reds pitcher-turned-broadcaster. "Here's what one of the paragraphs of that introduction would have sounded like if I hadn't taken out all the obscenities:

"I remember the BLEEPING time they brought in a BLEEP-BLEEPED model airplane guy. He had his BLEEP-ING gas planes diving and doing all kinds of BLEEPING stuff. He was buzzing the BLEEPING scoreboard with 'em, but he didn't get one of them up BLEEP-BLEEPED quick enough and whammm! Oh, man, I mean he BLEEPING smoked it. That BLEEP-BLEEPED plane BLEEPING broke into about 400 BLEEP-BLEEPED pieces."

When I was in Oakland, California, in 1987 to cover the 58th major league All-Star Game, I visited Richard Grossinger, who runs North Atlantic Books out of his house in Berkeley. Grossinger is an important figure in baseball literature, having published several anthologies of literary baseball pieces, including the seminal *Baseball I Gave You All the Best Years of My Life*. Richard and I had an enjoyable chat, and when it was time for me to go he generously loaded me up with gift copies of books his press had published. The last book he handed me was *Io #10*, the baseball issue of "a journal exploring myth, geography, origins, and the common source materials of literature, natural history, and physical science." *Io #10* had been published in 1971 and was a precursor of *Baseball I Gave You All the Best Years of My Life*.

"I get calls all the time from people who are desperately looking for this book," said Grossinger. "These callers are fans of a very famous writer, and they want this book because it contains the very first thing the writer ever published. I don't have any copies of it to sell—I'm giving you the last extra copy I have—but I get a little irritated because these people try to put one over on me. They pretend that they don't know the book is worth a lot of money."

I thanked Richard for the book and, highly intrigued, turned to the table of contents. There I saw listed a baseball poem titled "Brooklyn August," written by none other than Stephen King. Yes, *that* Stephen King.

OIL CAN BOYD

In 1984 the Boston Red Sox had three young pitchers who were enjoying their first success in the big leagues: Al Nipper, Roger Clemens, and Dennis "Oil Can" Boyd. Nipper wound up having a mediocre career; Clemens went on to become a genuine star; and Boyd . . . well, his modest success as a hurler was completely overshadowed by his bizarre antics and statements, which were in evidence right from the beginning.

To wit: the trio of pitchers were lounging around the Red Sox bullpen one day when Nipper decided that the three of them as a group needed a nickname.

"How about 'The Three Stooges'?" asked Nipper.

"Forget it," said Clemens. "Leave me out of that."

"I got one," said Boyd. "Let's call ourselves 'Ma and Pa Kettle.'"

"'Ma and Pa Kettle'?" said Nipper. "I don't get it. Besides, it's only two names. How can we use that?"

"No, no, no," explained Boyd. "You're Ma [Nipper] . . . he's Pa [Clemens] . . . and I'm the kettle because I'm black."

GENE BRABENDER

In a 1971 spring training game, the Tokyo Orion ball club loaded the bases against California Angels pitcher Gene Brabender. Angels manager Lefty Phillips strolled out to the mound and delivered the following ultimatum to Brabender: "Get this next guy or I'll be back with a weather report."

"What's a 'weather report'?" asked Brabender.

"For you, it could be showers," replied the smiling Phillips.

Gene is the same player whose antics caused *New York Times* sportswriter George Vecsey to formulate "Brabender's Law," which stipulates that "the most inactive player during the World Series will be the most active during the clubhouse follies." Brabender never got off the Baltimore Orioles' bullpen bench during the 1966 World Series, but after the O's won Game 4 to sweep the Los Angeles Dodgers, he went nuts during the team's victory celebration, spraying champagne all over teammates as well as sportswriters, baseball officials, and innocent bystanders.

BOBBY BRAGAN

One of baseball's all-time good guys, Bobby Bragan, tells the following story about his days as the manager of the Milwaukee and Atlanta Braves.

"Joe Torre was catching for us one day when the opposing team had a runner on third base. The batter hit a grounder to short, and the runner on third broke for home. Our shortstop fielded the ball cleanly and threw a strike to Torre standing in front of the plate. The runner was out by 15 feet, but for some reason Torre didn't reach down and tag him, so the runner slid in safe. Joe didn't argue or complain to the umpire, so I didn't either, but I thought something strange was going on.

"After we got out of the inning and Torre was back in the dugout, I went up to him and said, 'Joe, it looked like we had that guy dead to rights . . . what in the world happened?'

"Torre said, 'Bobby, I just lost my nerve. I froze up, and I couldn't put the tag on him.'

"Well, the game went on and I forgot about that play, but looking back on it now, I realize that that was the origin of . . . Chicken Cacciatore."

GEORGE BRETT

Listen to Dan Quisenberry (former ace reliever of the Kansas City Royals) talk about George Brett, and you get the sense that Brett was not only a great hitter and the best all-around player in Royals history, but also a character with Ruthian qualities.

"George was a partyer who loved to stay out all night with the guys," says Quisenberry. "He hung with the backups because they didn't have to take the field the next day.

"One day in the early eighties we were playing in Texas, and it felt like the temperature was about a million degrees. George came into the clubhouse looking like a mess. His eyes were bloodshot, and his clothes were all wrinkled. You could tell he hadn't gotten much sleep, and he probably hadn't even taken off his clothes for the little bit of sleep he did get. All George did was hit three home runs in the game. Not only that, he called one of them.

"A submariner named Bob Babcock got George to pop up, and when George got back to the bench he said, 'If that guy throws me another sinker, middle of the plate and in, I'm going to hit it out there.' As he said this, he pointed to the bleachers in right center. The next time up, Babcock threw the same pitch in the same place and . . . boom! George hit it out of the park, right where he said he would.

"George also hit the most clutch home run I every saw, the home run that clinched the 1980 League Championship Series for us against the New York Yankees. We were winning

DON
POLLARD

the Series 2–0 but losing Game 3 2–1, with two on and two outs in the top of the seventh. Goose Gossage came in to relieve Tommy John, and it was like he was God. At that stage of his career Gossage was almost unhittable. New York knew they had us just where they wanted us, and their fans were going crazy.

"Well, George homered off Gossage, just crushed the ball, to put us up 4–2, and we went on to win the game by that score. We were all going nuts for a few minutes, but then the dugout got quiet as everybody was thinking about what George's home run meant: that we were going to the World Series for the first time in the franchise's history.

"Although I don't think many guys were thinking about it right then, it also meant nice World Series checks for all of us players and anybody else we as a team would normally vote a share of the money to, such as the team's trainer and equipment manager. Our equipment manager was a guy named Al Zych, or 'Bub,' as we called him, who always drove around in a clunker.

"At this point, when everybody in the dugout was in a reflective mood for a few moments, George turned to Zych and said, 'Bub, now you can get rid of that piece of crap you drive and buy something nice.'"

Brett obviously had a lot of physical ability, but according to Quisenberry what made him great was his intensity and incredible competitiveness.

"One night we were playing in Kansas City, and it was so humid you'd sweat just breathing. George struck out and was so mad about it he went into the runway connecting the dugout to the clubhouse and started beating up this big rubber garbage can full of trash with his bat. He worked himself into a real lather, and when he'd finally worked out his frustration he dropped the bat and just plopped himself down into the garbage can, totally exhausted.

"Another time we were playing in Detroit, and Milt Wilcox was pitching for the Tigers. George was batting in the middle of the game, and Milt knocked him down. George got up madder than hell—you could see that big jaw of his jutting out—and blasted the next pitch over the right-field wall, but foul. And he was mad about that.

"Well, Milt decked him again!

"A couple of pitches later George flied out to deep center, and as he rounded first he just couldn't stand it any longer. He sprinted toward Wilcox on the mound with murder in his eyes. The fly-out wasn't sufficient: he had to go fight him. One of the umpires, Ken Kaiser, saw it coming and got between George and Wilcox before either of them landed any punches, but it was still an unforgettable, frenzied, gladiator moment.

"And then there's this story which sounds unbelievable, but I think it's true because I heard it from several people.

"George was out golfing with a Boston writer on an off-day in the 1980 season, the year he hit over .400 for most of the summer. George was on the edge of the green, with the writer about 100 yards back. The writer hit a low shot that was flying like a missile right at George. The writer hollered, 'Look out!' but even as he did, George grabbed his golf club by the head, swung it like a baseball bat, and hit the golf ball right back toward the writer. As I said, I think this really happened, because when I asked George about it, he sort of grinned and said, 'Yeah, I really had it going that year.'"

BROADCASTERS

K en Levine, who has broadcast games for the Orioles, Mariners, and Padres, had another interesting career before he got into baseball. Levine wrote for and produced several hit television shows, including *M*A*S*H* and *Cheers*. The sense of humor Levine needed to make those sitcoms funny is evident in this story about his minor league broadcasting days.

"When I was broadcasting for the Syracuse Chiefs, the station that carried the games had a very weak signal. It didn't go very far at all, especially at night, and that was when most of our games were played, of course.

"One of the zany things I did to poke fun at our weak signal and to liven up our broadcasts was to pretend that we were merely the flagship station for a much larger network that broadcast to foreign countries all over the world. I'd say, 'Good evening, ladies and gentlemen, and welcome to the Syracuse Chiefs International Broadcasting Network.' And every night I'd welcome a new country to our network.

"Now, at the time, Syracuse had a third baseman named Norm Tonucci. He was a sweet kid but not a very good ballplayer. When he hit the ball it went a long way, but he struck out a lot and had a lot of "O-fers."

"Anyway, one night I said that Borneo was the latest foreign country to join our network, all because of Norm Tonucci. I made up this whole scenario that Tonucci was a big name there because his father had been a big war hero, had saved a lot of people from the Japanese during World War II.

According to me, Tonucci had a big fan club in Borneo, and there were lots of little kids running around there named 'Norm.' Tonucci played along and even did some promos: 'This is Norm Tonucci, and I'd like to say hi to all my fans in Borneo.' He liked the attention.

"One night not long after this we were playing a series-opening game in Oklahoma City. We had had a long game the night before and had taken an early-morning flight out of Syracuse, so I hadn't gotten much sleep and was kind of punchy. Tonucci, though, was in rare form. First time up, he hit a triple, and after I described the play I said, 'They're going crazy in the streets of Borneo over what's happening here at All Sports Stadium!'

"Tonucci's second time up, he swung at the first pitch and really got ahold of one. I mean, he hit one to the moon.

"And my home-run call was: 'Tonucci hits a long drive to left . . . Steve Kemp is back at the wall . . . he looks up . . . *there's no school tomorrow in Borneo!*'"

Longtime Minnesota Twins radio announcer Herb Carneal says that he made a big mistake when he got married. Not in marrying Mrs. Carneal, but rather in the timing of the wedding, which took place when he was broadcasting minor league games in Springfield, Massachusetts.

"My wife and I got married on September 12," says Herb. "We didn't have sense enough to get married after the season, so that now we can't do anything but go to a ball game on our anniversary."

Elvis Presley continues to have a curious hold over the imaginations of many Americans. At least once a year, or so it seems, the tabloids report that Elvis has been seen alive and well in a shopping mall or doughnut shop. Eventually, Elvis was going to be seen at a major league ballpark, and it happened in 1996 at Cincinnati's Riverfront Stadium.

It all started innocently enough. Dave Armbruster, producer of the Reds' radio broadcasts for station wlw, found a photo he thought paired an interesting couple: Elvis and former president Richard M. Nixon. Armbruster showed the photo to Reds play-by-play man Marty Brennaman, and Brennaman was so struck by it that he declared 1996 "The Year of the King" in the Reds' radio booth. He announced this over the air and invited Elvis fans to send in Elvis photos and memorabilia with which to decorate the radio booth.

Reds fans took the bait, and before long the wlw radio booth at Riverfront was transformed into an Elvis shrine, with Elvis's image adorning towels, wall hangings, velvet paintings, and an entire bulletin board full of photos, postcards, and newspaper clippings. The centerpiece of this tribute to the King was a large painted ceramic Elvis bust, which Brennaman proudly set out on the windowless ledge of his broadcast booth for all to see and enjoy before each game.

The story might have ended here if not for the Reds players, for whom the Elvis bust was too much of a temptation.

On three different occasions during pregame warm-ups Reds players took aim at Elvis, firing baseballs from the home-plate area toward the wlw radio booth three decks above the playing field. Elvis escaped harm the first two days but wasn't so lucky on the third day.

On May 8, 1996, as his teammates lay on the ground stretching, burly Reds catcher Joe Oliver let go throw after throw. Whenever one of his long, arching throws whizzed past

Elvis's sideburns or banged into the concrete facade beneath him, Oliver's teammates emitted groans of disappointment. Oliver never did shatter Elvis, but he did hit him squarely with a ricochet of his fortieth or so throw, which knocked a chunk of plaster out of the King's left shoulder.

The good-natured Brennaman didn't get bent out of shape over Oliver's vandalism; on the other hand, he decided not to put Elvis on display any longer until shortly before game time. Explaining his new policy, Brennaman said, "Elvis has survived three assassination attempts. I won't expose him to another one. Long live the King."

Brennaman's strategic retreat did not satisfy the Reds, who decided, once they had fallen into last place in the National League's Central Division, that Elvis had been bringing them bad luck. Prior to their game on June 4, with their season record standing at 21–30, the entire Reds team met Reds president and CEO Marge Schott in her office and demanded that the ceramic jinx go.

Brennaman acceded to the players' wishes, as Schott directed him to, but this time he expressed nothing but scorn for the players' attitude: "If they have to blame the radio booth for the fact that they're off to their worst start in 25 years, that's pretty weak."

JAY BUHNER

Some baseball promotions are readily transferrable from one team to another. Take Bat Day, for example—that works anywhere.

Other baseball promotions are not readily transferrable. Such as Jay Buhner Buzz Cut Night. That's one Seattle Mariners promotion other major league teams are not likely to copy.

Buhner is the Mariners' slugging rightfielder whose popularity derives in part from his razor-cut "hair-less" style. On July 23, 1996, the Mariners gave away free tickets to their game against the Milwaukee Brewers to any fans willing to have their head shaved à la Buhner. The Mariners' barbers were busy as a total of 3,321 fans, including 28 women, took advantage of the offer. Said the approving Buhner, "It's a good look for the summer."

One sure sign of baseball's popularity is the frequency with which TV sitcoms refer to major league teams and players and the confidence the writers and producers of the shows have that the viewing public will catch the significance of the references.

Seinfeld is one such show that loves to rub elbows with baseball. In fact, *Seinfeld* developed a plotline around lovable loser George Costanza's landing a front-office job with the New York Yankees. In one of the episodes involving this highly improbable and comic plotline, George believes, because his contributions to the Yankees organization are so minimal, that no one will even notice his absence as he takes an unauthorized vacation; however, the Yankees do notice his absence and conclude that George is dead.

Yankees owner George Steinbrenner (actually, the actor who portrays Steinbrenner on the show) visits the home of George's parents and delivers the horrible news. George's parents are momentarily stunned, but Mr. Costanza, keenly aware of whom he is talking to, recovers and shouts: "How could the Yankees trade Jay Buhner? No wonder they can't win the pennant!"

CASEY CANDAELE

Tommy Kramer, who went 7–3 lifetime with the Cleveland Indians, had one unforgettable moment of glory in the major leagues. On May 24, 1993, Kramer pitched a complete-game one-hitter against the Texas Rangers at Cleveland's Municipal Stadium. Julio Franco's fourth-inning home run spoiled not only Kramer's no-hitter and shutout, but also his perfect game, as no other Ranger reached base that night.

In 1994 Kramer became teammates with Casey Candaele as both of them played for the Triple A Indianapolis Indians. Candaele, who'd spent time in the big leagues with the Montreal Expos and Houston Astros, had a most unusual baseball background. It wasn't his father who'd been a professional baseball player before him, but rather his mother, the former Helen St. Aubin, who had played in the All-American Girls Baseball League that began during World War II and was celebrated in the movie *A League of Their Own*. Candaele also had a well-deserved reputation for being a flake. According to Kramer the Indians never knew what Candaele would do next, but he was especially unpredictable and prone to pranks in airports, where he would do zany things to help alleviate the boredom.

"We had just flown into Buffalo," says Kramer, "and we were sitting around waiting for our luggage. We had a couple of vans waiting outside to take us to our hotel downtown.

"Candaele notices some Barney Fife–type security guards hanging around, so he puts on some sunglasses and starts walking very, very slowly toward the luggage carousel. He's walking on his toes like the San Diego Chicken does when he's sneaking up on the umpires. Every few feet he stops dead in his tracks and looks to the right and then to the left as if he's checking to see if the coast is clear. He's acting as mysteriously as possible, actually trying to draw the attention of the security guards.

"When Casey's certain that the security guards have noticed him and are watching his every move, he sprints up to the carousel, grabs his own bags, and runs like hell through the airport. The rent-a-cops, of course, take off after him. They're running through the airport, too, blowing their whistles and shouting at Casey to stop. The whole time we're laughing ourselves silly.

"They chase him all the way to one of our vans, where Casey pulls out ID, shows them the tags on his luggage, and proves that he hasn't stolen anything—or, more precisely, that he's stolen his own luggage!

"The rent-a-cops want to strangle Casey, but there's not much they can do."

STEVE CARLTON

In order to totally concentrate on his pitching, Steve Carlton put cotton in his ears before taking the mound. As far as sportswriters were concerned, Carlton could have left the cotton in his ears after the games were over. That's because Carlton adopted a vow of silence toward all members of the media in 1973 after he had become infuriated with the criticism of Philadelphia newspaper reporters. Even after the Phillies won the 1980 World Series (with a lot of help from Carlton), Steve refused to bury the hatchet; while his teammates celebrated and joyfully submitted to interviews in the Phillies' clubhouse, Carlton celebrated privately, sipping champagne in the trainer's room, which is always off-limits to the media.

As his career fizzled out in the late 1980s—he played for five teams in two years—Carlton finally relented and began to talk to reporters, telling them of his love of baseball and his belief that he could still pitch effectively in the big leagues. One reporter couldn't resist commenting on the irony of the timing. "Carlton finally learned to say hello when it was time to say good-bye," he said.

Carlton's last-minute mellowing didn't exactly transform him into a candidate for any team's Good Guy Award, given to players who are especially cooperative with the media. Steve spent his last go-round with the Minnesota Twins, for whom he posted a 1–6 record in 1987–88. In late August of 1987, Carlton was sitting in the visitors' dugout at Boston's Fenway Park when a radio reporter asked him if they could do a brief interview about his 300th win, which he had earned in 1983 while still with the Phillies.

Carlton's reply was: "You know, I'd like to. But, see, I had this terrible car accident about a year ago, and I don't remember anything about my career. Sorry."

ROGER CLEMENS

Roger Clemens and his brother Randy have always been close. Randy was a terrific amateur athlete and in the early days of Clemens's professional career sometimes advised his younger brother on how to pitch. On one occasion Roger ignored big brother's words of wisdom and afterward wished that he hadn't.

In his rookie season with the Red Sox, Clemens was excited about pitching against slugger Reggie Jackson of the California Angels. Clemens felt that facing Jackson, legendary for his clutch power hitting, would be the ultimate test of his ability. Before the game Randy told Roger, "You're going to strike out the big-namers once or twice, but don't try to strike them out the third time, because they'll rise to the occasion."

Firing his 96-mph fastball, Clemens fanned Jackson once, then twice. On Jackson's third appearance, with the Red Sox down 1–0 and a man on first, the count went to 2–2. Clemens considered pitching Jackson away but decided to challenge him one more time. Roger threw his best fastball down the middle, and Reggie, as if on cue, deposited it in the Fenway Park bleachers. As Jackson trotted around the bases, Clemens glanced into the stands and saw his brother standing with his arms spread apart as if to say, "Didn't I tell you not to do that?"

FLEA CLIFTON

One of baseball's most popular arguments revolves around the question "Who was the fastest pitcher of all time?" The following story won't settle the debate once and for all, but it sure does score a few points in favor of a certain pitcher always championed by some as the fastest pitcher ever. The story is told by Herman "Flea" Clifton, a reserve infielder for the Detroit Tigers from 1934 through 1937.

"The first time we played the Cleveland Indians during my rookie year," says Clifton, "I went out to watch the Indians take batting practice. I wanted to see them hit because they had some people who could swing the bat . . . Hal Trosky, Earl Averill, Sam Rice, Joe Vosmik.

"Well, I was sitting there in our dugout, and to my surprise these guys weren't hitting nothing. This big old plowboy was out there pitching, and the Indians could hardly hit a foul tip off him, in batting practice. This plowboy was throwing with a nice and easy sidearm motion, but the ball was just exploding up to the plate.

"Our manager, Mickey Cochrane, and one of his coaches, Cy Perkins, came into the dugout, so I said to them, 'Who's that plowboy out there pitching? The Indians can't even hit a foul ball off him.'

"Cochrane looked at Perkins, and Perkins looked at Cochrane, and then they both laughed. 'You don't know who that is?' asked Cochrane.

" 'No, I don't. That's why I'm asking you,' I said.

" 'That's Walter Johnson,' Cochrane said.

" 'Walter Johnson!' I said. 'He's the Cleveland manager; he's got to be almost 50 years old; and his own pitchers don't throw that fast?!'

" 'And I'm damn glad they don't,' said Cochrane."

COLLECTING

You know baseball card collecting has become a national obsession when a dispute over the transaction of a single card that involves a juvenile winds up in court.

One of the most notorious cases in baseball card jurisprudence began when 12-year-old Bryan Wrzensinski went card shopping at the Ball-Mart card shop in Ithaca, Illinois. Peering into one of the store's glass showcases, Bryan noticed an interesting item: a $1,200 Nolan Ryan rookie card bearing a price sticker with the decimal in the wrong place. Sensing an opportunity to acquire the treasured card at a price that fit his Little League budget, Bryan asked the clerk on duty, a temporary employee with scant knowledge of cards and their values, how much the card was. When the clerk said, "Twelve dollars," Bryan made the purchase and went happily on his way.

Of course, word of Bryan's great buy spread quickly, and it wasn't long before shop owner Joe Irmen contacted Bryan's father. Irmen explained that the price of the card had been a mistake and demanded that the card be returned for a refund. Mr. Wrzensinski said a deal's a deal. Irmen said, "I'll see you in court."

In the meantime, baseball card magazine commentators had a blast analyzing the situation, most of them arguing that regardless of the legality of the purchase it was probably not ethical for the buyer to keep the card, while also admitting that they thought most hobbyists would have done the same thing as young Wrzensinski.

The trial, which began in early March of 1991 before Judge Ann Jorgensen, quickly degenerated into a shouting match that caused Jorgensen to clear the courtroom after the Wrzensinskis' lawyer revealed that Bryan had traded the contested card the night before for a 1965 Joe Namath football card and a 1967 Tom Seaver rookie card. Jorgensen eventually persuaded the litigants to reach a settlement sans attorneys. Under the compromise Wrzensinski was to revoke the Ryan-for-Namath/Seaver trade, return the Ryan card to Irmen, and get back his $12; Irmen was then to auction off the Ryan rookie and turn over the proceeds to charity.

Since Judge Jorgensen didn't make a ruling, it didn't exactly turn out to be a precedent-setting case; however, it did reemphasize and refine a business truism in regard to the seemingly innocent baseball card marketplace: Let the buyer and seller beware!

As interest in baseball card collecting exploded in the 1980s, more and more companies not in the baseball card business per se tried to boost sales of their product by offering baseball cards as premiums. In 1991 the Borden Company caused baseball card collectors around the country to rediscover Cracker Jack by including a miniature 1991 Topps baseball card as the "toy surprise" in each box. The miniature cards, exactly one-fourth the size of Topps' regular cards, were issued in two series of 36 and were available only in boxes of Cracker Jack.

Did the promotion help Borden sell more Cracker Jack? Well, judging by the actions of collector Tol Broome of

Greensboro, North Carolina, it certainly did. Broome and helpful relatives purchased 108 boxes of Cracker Jack in an attempt to complete the first series of cards. This was more Cracker Jack than the Broome household could stomach, so Broome took bowls of the sweetened popcorn and peanut snack to work for fellow employees to munch on in the company lunchroom.

Even after raiding 108 boxes, Broome wound up one card short of a full set of 36 and had to trade with another collector to acquire his final card, that of the Cardinals' Pedro Guerrero. With Cracker Jack retailing at 3 boxes for $1, the 108 boxes cost Broome and family more than $35 . . . something to remember the next time a company entices you to buy its product with an offer of free baseball cards.

As every baseball card collector knows, the wackiest player notes have always appeared on the backs of cards produced by Topps, the most famous and the oldest of current baseball card manufacturers. Veteran collectors have learned not to expect the comments on every Topps card to describe an outstanding performance or a highlight of the player's career. Sometimes the comments aren't particularly flattering either, or even baseball-related, for that matter.

For instance, the back of Mike Pagliarulo's 1987 card says that "Mike attends Boston Celtics and Bruins games." Imagine that . . . a professional athlete who enjoys watching other professional sports.

The 1991 card of Cardinals shortstop–second baseman Jose Oquendo says that "Jose is regularly the first player at park for game." (Things at home are that bad, eh, Jose?)

As for publicizing something to make Mom and Dad proud, how about the comment on the back of Dodgers first baseman Mike Marshall's 1985 card: "Mike has been nicknamed 'Big Foot' because he wears a size 14 shoe."

For sheer irrelevance (not to mention atrocious grammar), though, it would be tough to top the scintillating revelations found on the back of pitcher Tom Niedenfuer's 1989 card: "Born in Minnesota, Tom's family moved to Pennsylvania when he was age three. He resided in Scranton and West Chester, then moved to Washington State in third grade." Wow! Who else but a Topps copywriter could have packed so much inside dope on a major league pitcher into two measly sentences.

Major league ballplayers are generally suspicious of favor-seeking fans, so when David Drozen of Calabasas, California, decided he wanted one of Dave Winfield's game-used fielder's gloves, he made a proposition, not a request. Back in 1991 Drozen owned a jazz recording company. He knew that Winfield loved jazz, so he wrote the big outfielder a letter outlining his trade proposal: one hundred jazz CDs for a game-used Winfield ball glove. Shortly afterward an incredulous Drozen found himself talking to a cautious Winfield, who said, "I read your letter, and I decided that if you were a gentleman and this was really your company, then I would go ahead and make this trade."

After Drozen consummated his deal with Winfield, he made the same offer to Andre Dawson, who also accepted it after verifying its legitimacy. In addition to a game-used glove, Dawson sent Drozen a game-used cap and batting glove.

Drozen was so taken with his two gloves that he sold his music business in order to become a full-time glove dealer. He has since acquired numerous gloves that once belonged to stars such as Harmon Killebrew, Reggie Jackson, Carlton Fisk, Bill Buckner, Roger Clemens, and Ken Griffey Jr., and he is now widely known as one of the country's leading glove collectors and experts.

Sports memorabilia hobbyists sometimes get carried away, buying and selling items of no real sports significance except that they were once possessed by or connected to a ballplayer. For example, a few years ago a baseball memorabilia auction included among its offerings an autographed commissary ticket that Pete Rose had redeemed during his incarceration at an Illinois federal prison. Pretty silly, but nothing compared with Mickey Mantle's Oklahoma boyhood home.

That's right . . . not a door knocker or a mailbox or a weather vane that had been attached to the Mantle house, but rather the entire house itself. Lelands auction house offered the modest four-room dwelling in a 1994 auction, and it actually sold, too, for $55,000 ($60,500 once the buyer's premium was factored in). The clincher must have been that the house included a backyard tin barn that, according to the Lelands catalog, was "battered with marks and dents from Mantle's early pitching and batting sessions."

The two California collectors who bought the house said they planned to move it to a tourist area, such as Las Vegas, Nevada, or Branson, Missouri, and turn the place into a Mickey Mantle museum. The new owners admitted that they didn't have much Mantle memorabilia to put into their museum yet but were hoping to find "if they're out there, the original couches, beds, etc., from the house."

No word on what the wives of the collectors who bought the house said (or did!) upon learning of their husbands' successful bid.

SCOTT COOPER

Hitting for the cycle—hitting a single, double, triple, and home run, in any order, in a single game—is so rare a feat that many a ballplayer has been tempted to give up an extra base in order to achieve it. Scott Cooper of the Boston Red Sox didn't intentionally pass up an inside-the-park home run in order to complete his cycle, but he was lucky, artistically speaking, to get thrown out at home.

Cooper's cycle came in a 22–11 blowout of the Royals in Kansas City on April 12, 1994. In the top of the third inning with two outs and the Bosox already ahead 9–1, Cooper smashed a ball down the left-field line that looked as if it would be a routine stand-up double. Cooper jogged into second, but as leftfielder Vince Coleman raced toward the corner, the ball ricocheted past him back into left field. Cooper shifted back into high gear and sprinted toward third, where he enjoyed only a few moments' rest before he was waved home by coach Andy Allanson.

The fatigued Cooper dutifully staggered on but was tagged out easily as he slid into home, where he lay laughing and gasping for breath. The Red Sox didn't miss the run, and the triple Cooper was credited with turned out to be exactly what he needed to get his name into the record books.

COOPERSTOWN

Because it's the home of the National Baseball Hall of Fame and Museum, Cooperstown, New York, is a magical place for baseball fans, and it's not surprising that a lot of good baseball stories come out of the picturesque little village located in mid-state New York.

The Hall of Fame is located in Cooperstown because Cooperstown is where, according to legend, Abner Doubleday invented baseball. The Doubleday story was proven some time ago to be a myth, but few people at this point would like to see the Hall of Fame located anywhere but Cooperstown. Still, the locals feel obligated to defend the legend, and no one has done it any better than Wendell Tripp, who told the following story when he delivered his first speech at the Hall of Fame induction ceremonies as mayor of Cooperstown:

"Welcome to Cooperstown, the birthplace of baseball. When I say this, that Cooperstown is the birthplace of baseball, some of you may snicker and some of you may even hold your sides and fall on the ground with laughter, because some sportswriters when they don't have anything else to write about dispute this in their columns.

"But you may know that there was an eyewitness to the birth of baseball here in Cooperstown, a local man named Abner Graves who knew the founder of baseball, Abner Doubleday. Graves testified at the Mills Commission, which had been formed to investigate the origin of baseball. A few years later Albert Goodwill Spalding wrote a book called *America's National Game* in which he repeated Graves's testimony and the findings of the Mills Commission, which identified Cooperstown as the official birthplace of baseball.

"Spalding sent copies of his book to the White House as a gift for William Howard Taft and to the Vatican as a gift for Pope Pius X. And neither of these men sent back a letter disputing what was in Spalding's book.

"And if what Graves said is good enough for the President of the United States and for His Holiness the Pope, then it's good enough for me!"

Baseball stories come even from the pulpits of the churches of Cooperstown. Father John Sice of St. Mary's Catholic Church delights in telling what happened one year when Father Flynn came over from Ireland to stay in Cooperstown at St. Mary's for the summer:

"Induction Weekend came around, and as Father Flynn had no knowledge of baseball, I wanted to take him to the Hall of Fame Game, which is played between one National League team and one American League team on Monday, the day after the inductions. The only problem was that the game was all sold out.

"So at Mass that Sunday morning I made a plea during my sermon: 'Wouldn't it be a shame if the priests of St. Mary's, who are very good baseball fans, couldn't attend the game on Monday?'

"After Mass I went out to run some errands, and when I came back Father Flynn said, 'Father John, we've had some visitors. A tall man with glasses came to the door and left us tickets to the ball game. He had a funny name, Boo-some-thing-or-other.'

" 'You mean "Bowie"?'

" 'Yes, that's it,' said Father Flynn. The tall man, of course, was Bowie Kuhn, the commissioner of baseball.

" 'Another man came to the door, and he had tickets for us too,' said Father Flynn. 'His name sounded like "garage."'

"That was Joe Garagiola.

"Later on we had more visitors, and they all brought us tickets, so that by the end of the day we had enough tickets that we could have opened our own ticket booth."

R alph Kiner was a slugging outfielder who won seven consecutive National League home-run titles from 1946 to 1952. As a player Kiner uttered one of baseball's pithiest sayings: "Home-run hitters drive Cadillacs; singles hitters drive Fords." The remark could have been a nice verbal legacy for Kiner had he kept his mouth shut; instead, as a radio and TV announcer for the New York Mets, he has demonstrated such a penchant for malapropisms and non sequiturs that his verbal slipups have become known as "Kinerisms."

It was Kiner who said, "If Casey Stengel were alive today, he'd be spinning in his grave" as well as "All the Mets' road wins against Los Angeles this year have been at Dodger Stadium."

Thus, when Ralph was called upon to introduce broadcaster Bob Wolff, who was to receive the Ford C. Frick Award at the 1995 Hall of Fame induction ceremonies, I looked forward to hearing a new "Kinerism." Kiner spoke without incident for a couple of minutes, but then he delivered as anticipated. To set up his remarks about Wolff's stint as a TV broadcaster of Washington Senators games, Kiner attempted to repeat an old joke about the Senators; however, what he said was that Washington "was first in war, first in peace, and last in the *National* League." 'Atta boy, Ralph!

PAT DARCY

When Sparky Anderson managed the Cincinnati Reds, he earned the nickname "Captain Hook" for being so quick to go to his bullpen. In 1975 when the Reds won their division by 20 games, Cincinnati pitchers turned in a measly 23 complete games, the lowest figure in the majors (Yankees and Orioles pitchers tied for the major league lead with 70 complete games).

At one point during that season the Reds' pitching staff set a new major league record for most consecutive games without a complete game. The local papers made a big deal of the streak, and the players, as well as everyone who followed the team, were keenly aware of it.

Right-hander Pat Darcy finally broke the streak by going the distance (for his only complete game of the season) on an extremely hot and muggy night. Sportswriter Bob Hertzel was impressed that Darcy was able to pitch the full nine innings in such heat, to which some of the spectators had succumbed.

"Great job, Pat!" he said. "Did you know there were people fainting in the stands?"

"Just because I pitched a complete game?" asked an incredulous Darcy.

DELINO DESHIELDS

When second baseman Delino DeShields broke in with the Montreal Expos in 1990, he decided to make a fashion statement, with a purpose. Bucking the trend of wearing one's uniform with pants legs down to the ankles, DeShields wore his pants at the knees, with plenty of stirrup socks showing, as a way of paying tribute to the players of the old Negro Leagues.

Early in the 1994 season DeShields (by then a member of the Los Angeles Dodgers) began to experience circulation problems below the knees because of his old-time style of dress, and he started wearing his pants like everyone else.

Until, that is, his family saw him play. They objected strenuously to Delino's abandonment of his tribute, and at their urging he hiked his pants back up to continue it. "I didn't realize how important it was to other people," said DeShields.

DeShields's fashion statement didn't exactly catch on the way batting gloves did in the 1970s, but it won at least one convert to the cause, Dodgers outfielder Raul Mondesi, who won the National League Rookie of the Year Award in 1994. It also mattered to the honorees: "I haven't heard from Negro League players directly," said DeShields, "but I've heard through others that they appreciate it."

ROB DIBBLE

Rob Dibble was a hard-throwing Cincinnati Reds relief pitcher who could control his fastball but not his temper. Dibble's childish outbursts embarrassed himself and the Reds on numerous occasions, including the time in April 1991 when, immediately following a difficult save, he hurled a baseball from the Riverfront Stadium pitcher's mound 400 feet into the center-field bleachers, where it struck a startled, pregnant elementary school teacher on the left elbow and then bounced into her husband's Coke. Dibble had pulled a similar stunt in the minors four years earlier. After catching a hard-hit liner to end the game, Dibble threw the baseball over the press box and completely out of Herschel Greer Stadium, home of the Triple-A Nashville Sounds.

Understandably, the Cincinnati press corps always tread lightly around Dibble. After the big pitcher had blown his third consecutive save opportunity in June of 1993, reporters approached Dibble's locker cautiously, expecting him to explode at any moment. Instead Dibble calmly lobbed the writers a change-up.

"I've got a joke for you," said Dibble. "Why was six afraid of seven?"

After one reporter answered incorrectly, Dibble said, "Wrong. Because seven eight [ate] nine. . . . I heard that on *Sesame Street*."

DON DRYSDALE

On the mound, Hall of Fame pitcher Don Drysdale was a fierce, even hated competitor, but off the field he was quite a different person. Tommy Lasorda likes to tell the following story to illustrate Drysdale's gentlemanly side.

In 1955 Drysdale was a rookie on the Dodgers' Triple A farm team in Montreal. His roommate was left-handed pitcher Tommy Lasorda, a six-year veteran of the club. One day the two Royals pitchers were out in public when a group of people recognized Lasorda and crowded around him for his autograph. "OK, but you better get his autograph too," said Lasorda, pointing to Drysdale. "That's Don Drysdale, and someday he's going to be pitching for the Dodgers."

In 1963 Lasorda had just moved out to the West Coast to begin his minor league managing career, while Drysdale was the toast of Los Angeles for having just helped the Dodgers sweep the New York Yankees in the World Series. A few days after the Series ended, Drysdale visited a local television station to be interviewed and asked Lasorda to tag along. When employees at the station besieged the World Series hero with autograph requests, Drysdale pointed toward Lasorda and said, "Fine, but you'd better get his autograph too. That's Tommy Lasorda, and someday he's going to be the Dodgers' manager."

Drysdale's reputation as a brushback pitcher—some would say "beanball pitcher"—was well deserved. In his 14-year career the 6'6" sidearmer hit 154 batters, a National League record. Drysdale not only intentionally hit batters, but also talked openly about it. He put his philosophy of retaliation this way: "If you knock down one of my guys, I knock down two of yours."

There is also an old baseball maxim about the inside half of home plate belonging to the hitter, with the outside half of the plate belonging to the pitcher. This maxim is meant to politely warn hitters against digging into the batter's box too deeply and leaning out over the plate to hit the outside pitch. Drysdale even put his own threatening spin on that: "Half the plate belongs to the batter, and half the plate belongs to me. That's fair. It's just that I never let the batter know which half is mine."

Drysdale beanball stories are numerous. Here's a good one that St. Louis Cardinals outfielder Lou Brock told Frank Dolson of the *Philadelphia Inquirer*. One day at Dodger Stadium, St. Louis catcher Gene Oliver blasted a long home run off Drysdale. Before beginning a leisurely trot around the bases, Oliver first stood at home plate admiring the flight of the ball and then said, loud enough for Drysdale to hear, "Hey, batboy, come get the bat."

Oliver's actions came under the heading of "showing up" the pitcher, and it was a foregone conclusion that Drysdale would make Oliver pay for his Cardinal sins. The next time Oliver batted, Drysdale drilled him with a fastball. While Oliver writhed in the dirt of the batter's box and teammates and the Cardinals' trainer rushed to his aid, Drysdale said loud enough for everyone to hear, "Hey, batboy, come get Oliver."

As if his intimidating size, overpowering fastball, sidearm delivery, and nasty disposition weren't enough to make National League batters miserable, Drysdale also threw a mean spitball.

After Drysdale quit pitching, he began a second career as a baseball radio broadcaster, working in that capacity for the California Angels, for the Chicago White Sox, and, finally, before his fatal heart attack in 1993, for his old team, the Los Angeles Dodgers. Shortly after Don started his stint with the Angels, someone asked California manager Gene Mauch how he thought Drysdale was doing as an announcer. Mauch, who had managed the Philadelphia Phillies during most of Drysdale's pitching career, said, "He talks pretty well for somebody who always had two fingers stuck in his mouth."

EBBETS FIELD

The New York Mets have provided a National League presence in the Big Apple since 1962, but they have never replaced the Brooklyn Dodgers in the hearts of the Dodgers' most loyal fans. To this day, the fans of "Dem Bums" mourn the loss of their beloved team, as well as the loss of the equally beloved home of the Brooklyn Dodgers, Ebbets Field, which was razed in 1960 to make way for a low-rent public housing project.

Brooklyn Dodgers fans have kept the spirit of the franchise alive by passing their favorite Dodgers stories down to the next generation, and pilgrimages of senior "Bums" fans taking junior "Bums" fans to the site where Ebbets Field once stood are not uncommon.

Brooklynite Bob Rosen once took his young son on such a pilgrimage. Rosen and son stood on the famous corner of Bedford Avenue and McKeever Place. Rosen pointed toward one of the high-rise public housing apartment buildings now occupying the site and said sadly, "That's where the Dodgers played."

"Which floor?" asked the son.

To Brooklyn Dodgers fans, everything about the team and Ebbets Field was special, including Tex Rickards, who served as the Ebbets Field public address announcer from 1924 through the end of the Dodgers' last season in Brooklyn in 1958. Although he had only an eighth-grade education, Rickards was the right man for the job because he spoke perfect "Brooklynese"; as Rickards told a group of English teachers intent on helping him improve his speech: "My people unastan what I say." (In 1957 *The Sporting News* published an article about Rickards titled "Fancy Woids Is for Da Boids.")

Over the years Rickards made a number of zany announcements at Ebbets Field, but none more memorable than what he said, or rather tried to say, on one very hot afternoon. Trying to keep cool, many of the fans in the front row of the center-field bleachers took off their coats and shirts and hung them over the railing. Realizing that this created a distraction for the batters, Rickards took the microphone and said, "Will the people sitting in the center-field boxes please take their clothes off . . ." Laughter from all parts of the ballpark drowned out the rest of the announcement.

BOB FELLER

If you don't think players pay attention to their own statistics, think again. The great ones, especially, are highly cognizant of the place in baseball history that their records make for them.

Consider what Bob Feller, the Cleveland Indians' great strikeout artist, said in June of 1996 to the learned members of the Society of American Baseball Research (SABR), gathered in Kansas City, Missouri, for their annual convention:

"Here's a fact about my career you guys might not know. I gave up 24 home runs with the bases loaded. When I got in a jam, I knew how to get out of it!

"I have a job for you SABR members. As you know, in 1946 I set a new American League record for strikeouts in a single season, with 348. At least, it was a record before some of you guys rummaged around in old score-books and somehow found seven more strikeouts for Rube Waddell, to give him a new total of 349 for the 1904 season.

"As you probably also know, I set the American League record for walks in 1938 with 208; Nolan Ryan walked 204 in 1977 for California. Now, go out there and find five more walks for Ryan!"

Feller also feels very protective toward the no-hitter he threw on Opening Day 1940, the only Opening Day no-no in baseball history.

"Every year, the day after Opening Day, my wife and I read the newspapers," says Feller, "and if nobody pitches a no-hitter, we wipe our brows and go, 'Whew!'"

CECIL FIELDER

You can understand it if Minnesota Twins pitcher Dan Naulty and catcher Greg Myers were not very concerned about the Detroit Tigers' Cecil Fielder's leading off first base after the huge slugger had drawn a walk to open the ninth inning of the April 2, 1996, game between the Tigers and Twins in the Minneapolis Metrodome. After all, this was Fielder's 1,097th major league game, and he had yet to steal a base, having been caught easily in all five of his previous attempts.

Nevertheless, one out later with a full count on Melvin Nieves and the Tigers leading 9–6, Tigers manager Buddy Bell flashed the sign . . . not the steal sign, but the hit-and-run sign, which was daring enough given the massive size of the human being who would be put in motion by the directive.

As Cecil lumbered toward second, Nieves swung at the pitch and missed for strike three. Greg Myers then fired the ball down to second. To no one's surprise it looked as if the throw would arrive in plenty of time to nail Cecil, but the ball nicked the sliding Fielder's helmet on the way in and kicked off the heel of shortstop Pat Meares's glove. Umpire Tim Tschida signaled "safe," and the official scorer ruled the play a stolen base. Fielder's record-setting streak of most games played without a stolen base had finally ended.

When it was announced over the public address system that this was Fielder's first major league stolen base, the Metrodome crowd went nuts. Some fans even bowed in mock homage, and Fielder thrust both arms skyward in a gesture of triumph.

After the game Fielder explained that getting his first stolen base had been only a matter of time: "I told you I was going to get one," he said. "I've been working on my jumps the last nine years. The pressure's off now. I'll go on from here. Buddy might start me moving a little more, now that he has seen me run."

After everyone stopped laughing at that last remark, Fielder added, "Hopefully, he won't."

Fielder's thievery shocked a lot of people, including the big man's wife, Stacey. She refused to believe that her husband had swiped a base until she saw the replay on ESPN's *Sports-Center* television show. Further helping to dispel Stacey's incredulity was the base itself, which was given to Cecil after the game as a memento. "I'll probably write the date on it and hang it up in my house," he said.

Fielder's once-in-a-lifetime heist brings to mind an even uglier stolen-base attempt by another giant slugger, Willie Stargell of the Pittsburgh Pirates. In his younger and skinnier days, Stargell had good wheels, but a succession of knee injuries and added weight robbed him of most of his speed and limited him to 17 stolen bases over his 21-year major league career.

It's hard to fathom what Pirates manager Chuck Tanner was thinking, but one day in 1978, when the Pirates were clobbering the Cubs in Chicago, Tanner ordered the 38-year-old Stargell to try to steal second.

Willie took off (so to speak) with the pitch and slid . . . but not into second base. In fact, Stargell hardly moved at all after his large body hit the dirt, and he came up about 10 feet short of the second-base bag. He stood up, and as Cubs shortstop Ivan DeJesus moved toward him to apply the tag, Stargell attempted to wiggle his way out of the predicament by making the "time-out" T sign with his hands. This bogus ploy was ignored by both DeJesus, who made the tag, and the umpire, who called Willie out.

Back in the dugout Stargell deadpanned the following explanation to his highly amused teammates: "I was given some bad information. I was told the bases were only 70 feet apart."

CHARLIE FINLEY

As owner of the Kansas City–Oakland A's franchise, Charlie Finley sometimes acted like a spoiled brat. A self-made millionaire and know-it-all, Finley constantly meddled with the managers of his ball clubs and had a serious problem accepting the authority of Commissioner Bowie Kuhn, whom he often called "the village idiot." Finley later amended that insult, saying, "I apologize to all the village idiots of America. He's the nation's idiot."

A tightwad throughout his tenure as owner of the A's franchise, Finley really ran a bare-bones operation prior to his sale of the team in 1981 to the Hass family of Levi Strauss fame. The new A's executives were aware that Finley, in anticipation of selling, had let the organization run down, but they were shocked on the first day of their regime to find out just how bush league the A's operation had become.

Wally Hass, the team's chief operating officer, was intent on stroking the front-office employees and making them feel wanted and needed. He decided to start with the receptionist, the first person he would see upon entering the A's offices. Hass's first pep talk was brief, because the receptionist turned out to be a cardboard sign that said, "Dial zero for assistance."

Undaunted, Hass thought he would send a letter of appreciation to the best A's fans, and so he asked the ticket manager to provide him a computer printout of season-ticket holders. To Hass's surprise, the ticket manager immediately complied with the request. The names of the A's season-ticket holders, all 75 of them, fit on one sheet of paper.

NELLIE FOX

Few players have been as respected by teammates and opponents alike as Nellie Fox, the highly competitive little second baseman of the Chicago White Sox who hustled and battled his way onto the American League All-Star team 11 different times in the 1950s and '60s. Despite his small stature (5'8", 160 pounds), Fox turned the double play fearlessly even when he knew some burly baserunner bearing down on him from first base was probably going to knock him into center field.

During a game against the Yankees in 1954, Fox was making the pivot on a double play when ex-Marine Hank Bauer barreled into him like an enraged rhino, after Nellie had already scampered several feet past the second-base bag, making it impossible for Fox to throw to first to complete the double play. Fox bounced up and protested to the umpire: "He [the batter-runner, then at first base] should be out for interference. Bauer came out of the baseline to get me."

Shaking his head and mumbling, "No, no, no," the umpire disagreed with Fox, so Nellie continued to press his case. White Sox manager Marty Marion rushed out onto the field to take up the argument and prevent Fox from being thumbed out of the game for arguing. Fox tried to reiterate his objection to the call, but Marion immediately snapped, "Stay out of it."

As Marion resumed his jawing with the immovable umpire, the Yankees' manager, Casey Stengel, made his way onto the scene to lend his support to the umpire's decision. Before

Stengel could open his mouth, the frustrated Fox said, "And what are you going to do, you old sonuvabitch? Tell a couple of funny stories?"

Four years later, on the same type of play, Bob Cerv of the Kansas City Athletics creamed Fox, leaving him with a couple of deep spike wounds and a wrenched knee. The gritty Fox finished out the inning and even played the next day, but his outraged teammates had had enough and were determined to get revenge.

Three Sox pitchers, Dick Donovan, Bill Fischer, and Bob Keegan, went to manager Al Lopez and begged for the next day's starting assignment, each desiring to be the one with the first opportunity to retaliate against Cerv. Lopez advised the trio that there was no need for them to volunteer, because the pitcher scheduled to work in rotation the next day was "quite adequate for the situation."

That pitcher was Early Wynn, one of the meanest, most notorious brushback pitchers of all time. The next day a couple of Wynn's beanball specials had Cerv rocking on his elbows in the batter's box and got the message through to him loud and clear: "Lay off little Nellie."

KEN GRIFFEY JR.

Some of baseball's oldest clubhouse pranks continue to work because they are most often pulled on unsuspecting rookies. Toward the end of spring training in 1989, Seattle Mariners manager Jim Lefebvre summoned rookie phenom Ken Griffey Jr., to his office. Griffey, who'd had a terrific spring, was expecting to hear that he'd officially made the team, but Lefebvre solemnly told him, "We've just traded you to Atlanta for Dale Murphy."

Griffey was stunned at this news and perplexed by its meaning. Had the Mariners given up on him? Did the Braves think he was already as good as two-time National League MVP Dale Murphy? Was he really going to have to leave all his friends in the Mariners organization and go down to Atlanta as a perfect stranger?

Lefebvre then asked the dazed youngster, "You know what day this is?"

As answers such as "major league cut-down day" and "inter-league trading deadline" flitted through Griffey's mind, the Seattle coaches burst into the room and shouted, "April Fool!"

The relieved Griffey not only made the team, but also played 127 games with such distinction that only injuries prevented him from winning the American League Rookie of the Year Award for 1989.

Griffey quickly went on to establish himself as one of baseball's premier superstars, but six years later he was still the object of pranks.

One day during spring training batting practice Griffey was really zoned in on the ball and was sending nearly every other pitch flying over the outfield fences. Seattle manager Lou Piniella leaned up against the batting cage and said, "Hey, Junior, I bet you a steak dinner you can't hit one of the next three pitches out of the park."

"You're on," said Griffey, who didn't come close to hitting one of pitcher Chris Bosio's next three servings out of the ball yard. What Griffey didn't know was that Piniella had arranged beforehand for Bosio to intentionally throw the "wagered" three pitches low and away, making it almost impossible for Griffey to hit them with the necessary power.

Although Griffey almost certainly suspected he'd been set up, he held up his end of the bet, in a manner of speaking. After the Mariners concluded their day of training, Piniella walked into his office and found his steak dinner waiting for him . . . in the form of a two-ton, foul-smelling, and somewhat irritated live steer!

"I like my steaks rare, but this is ridiculous," said a laughing Piniella.

One of the first entrepreneurs to capitalize on Ken Griffey Jr.'s enormous popularity was Mike Cramer of Pacific Trading Cards based in Edmonds, Washington. Before young Griffey's rookie season was half over in 1989, Cramer developed and marketed the Ken Griffey Jr. Milk Chocolate Bar.

Molded in the shape of a baseball card, the candy bar was so popular that Cramer could hardly keep up with demand. Griffey did not endorse the product, though, nor was there any danger of his eating his share of the profits: he's allergic to chocolate.

ALFREDO GRIFFIN

The Toronto Blue Jays' Alfredo Griffin was neither voted onto the American League 1984 All-Star team—he finished fourth in the voting at the shortstop position—nor selected to it by manager Joe Altobelli; yet being in the right place at the right time garnered a spot on the roster for him anyway. Here's how.

Starting American League shortstop Cal Ripken Jr., was supposed to be backed up by Detroit's Alan Trammell; however, Trammell hurt his elbow in the Tigers' last game before the All-Star break and was in no condition to participate in the big game to be played in San Francisco's Candlestick Park. Toronto's Damaso Garcia, who had been selected to the American League squad as a second baseman, asked his Dominican Republic countryman and double-play partner Griffin to go with him to San Francisco for the fun of it. Since the Blue Jays were to open the second half of the season in nearby Oakland, Griffin readily agreed. Milwaukee's Robin Yount had actually finished 382,624 votes ahead of Griffin in the balloting for the American League shortstop position, but when AL president Bobby Brown got word that Griffin was already in town, he contacted Griffin and asked if he would do Brown "the favor" of replacing Trammell on the American League team.

The next night Griffin suited up—Toronto's uniforms had already been shipped ahead to Oakland—and he even got to play, entering the game in the eighth inning as a defensive replacement for Ripken.

Griffin's impeccable timing also enabled him to socialize with the other Dominican All-Stars: Mario Soto (Reds), Juan Samuel (Phillies), Tony Pena (Pirates), and Rafael Ramirez (Braves). And then there was one final, unexpected reward. Griffin didn't know it, but a clause in his contract called for him to receive a bonus if he were to make the All-Star team. The day after the game the Blue Jays deposited a check for $25,000 into Griffin's bank account.

When Griffin was playing for the Los Angeles Dodgers, he pulled a fast one on the entire Dodger Stadium crowd when he substituted himself for another player.

In the last game of the 1990 season, Dodgers manager Tommy Lasorda pinch-ran for Eddie Murray after Murray knocked out his third base hit of the day. The fans gave Murray a standing ovation and continued their applause, demanding a curtain call, after Murray had returned to the dugout.

As Murray sauntered down the dugout, shaking hands with teammates, Griffin stuck his head out of the dugout, waved his cap to the crowd, and then returned to the bench. Satisfied that Murray had acknowledged their tribute, the crowd quieted down.

HARVEY HADDIX

On May 26, 1959, Pittsburgh Pirates left-hander Harvey Haddix pitched a perfect game for 12 innings, only to lose it all 2–0 . . . the perfect game, the no-hitter, and the ball game . . . in the bottom of the 13th on an error, a walk, and the Milwaukee Braves' first and only hit of the game, a double by first baseman Joe Adcock.

After the game a disconsolate Haddix received a two-word message in a telegram from a college fraternity. "Dear Harvey," it said, "Tough shit."

At first, Haddix was angry about the telegram, but after thinking about it for a few minutes he decided that the college boys had it exactly right.

WILD BILL HAGY

Fans usually don't become famous, but every Baltimore Orioles fan knows who Wild Bill Hagy is. With his long hair and flowing beard, the giant Hagy led Memorial Stadium crowds in cheers from atop the Orioles' dugout throughout the 1980s and became in the process something of a folk hero in Baltimore. Hagy's cohorts called themselves the "Section 34 Rowdies," and the Rowdies often followed the team on the road. Hagy recalls one time he and the Rowdies followed the Birds to New York.

"We had seats in Yankee Stadium that were in the same location as our seats back home," says Hagy. "During batting practice, Ken Singleton and Al Bumbry were shagging flies in the outfield. We hollered to Singleton, and he looked up and waved at us. Then he called over to Bumbry: 'Look who's here.' And Bumbry waved at us too.

"After the game we went into a bar across the street from Yankee Stadium to celebrate. There were about 80 of us. As soon as we started to walk in, the bartender said, 'No, no, no! You guys can't come in here.'

"I said, 'Now, wait a minute, man. Give us a chance.'

"I took a big cowboy hat that somebody had been wearing, and I went around and collected a dollar from everybody. Then I put this big stash of cash on the bar and said, 'Here's your tip in advance.'

"We got to stay, and not only that, 10 minutes later the bartender threw out two or three Yankees fans who had started mouthing off at us."

JAY HOOK

Right-handed pitcher Jay Hook had the dubious distinction of being an original New York Met, having been taken by the Mets in the expansion draft off the roster of the Cincinnati Reds. Years earlier Hook had graduated from Northwestern University with a degree in engineering, and he liked to expound in the bullpen on the aerodynamics of the curveball.

Mets manager Casey Stengel was aware of Hook's educational background and his reputation for having a genius-level IQ, but Stengel also knew that book smarts are of limited value on the baseball diamond. When Hook would not keep batters off balance by pitching inside as the Mets' crusty old manager urged his pitchers to do, Stengel said, "I've got the smartest pitcher in the world except when he's on the pitcher's mound."

Mets outfielder Richie Ashburn tells a Jay Hook story that proves the same point. The '62 Mets, it seems, were having a lot of trouble defending the double steal in first-and-third situations. Stengel called a team meeting to address the problem and asked if anybody had any suggestions. Hook raised his hand and said, "I've got an idea, Casey. When they try the double steal, why not have our pitcher intercept the throw down to second and then fire it back to the plate?" It sounded like a good plan, so the Mets agreed to try it.

As luck would have it, the next time the Mets were faced with a first-and-third situation, Hook was on the mound for the Mets, who were playing the Cincinnati Reds. The speedy

Vada Pinson was on first, while the plodding Wally Post was on third. Reds skipper Freddie Hutchinson put on the double steal, so as Hook delivered the next pitch both Pinson and Post began running. Mets catcher Choo Choo Coleman caught the pitch and fired a strike right over the pitcher's mound. Instead of intercepting Coleman's throw, Hook ducked and watched the ball fly toward second base. Mets second baseman Hot Rod Kanehl took the throw in front of the bag and made a great return throw that was on target and in time to nail the chugging Post—except that Hook, suddenly remembering the new plan, reached up and cut it off! . . . which allowed Post to score easily.

CHARLIE HOUGH

Texas Rangers knuckleballer Charlie Hough could have used the perspective of a telegram like Harvey Haddix's (see page 82) to "console" him for the way he lost a no-hitter on June 16, 1986.

Pitching in Anaheim, California, Hough took a no-hitter and a 1–0 lead into the bottom of the ninth against the Angels. After Charlie retired the Angels' leadoff man, pinch-hitter Jack Howell hit a fly ball down the left-field line. Left-fielder George Wright, a defensive replacement, who had been shading the left-handed–hitting Howell toward center field, raced over toward the foul line but wound up overrunning the ball, which bounced off the heel of his glove for a three-base error. Wally Joyner then singled to right center to break up the no-hitter and tie the score. After Joyner moved to second on a passed ball, Hough struck out third baseman Doug DeCinces for out number two and intentionally walked DH Reggie Jackson.

The inning should have ended when Hough struck out George Hendricks swinging on a 3–2 knuckleball, but catcher Orlando Mercado let the ball get by him for his second passed ball of the inning. Hough assumed Mercado would throw to first to complete the strikeout, but the ball rolled too far away from the plate for that. Seeing Hough standing like a statue on the pitcher's mound, Joyner, who had started the play on second, continued around third and crossed the unguarded plate with the winning run.

Despite pitching a one-hitter, Hough blamed himself for the loss. "It's 100 percent my fault," he said. "All I've got to do is walk to the plate. The most that can happen is he'll throw it to first and I'll have walked a few feet for nothing." Angels manager Gene Mauch, a 40-year veteran of professional baseball, put this spin on the bizarre ninth inning: "That was the most unique finish to a game I've ever seen. I've seen them all kinds of ways, but never with a guy scoring from second on a strikeout and a passed ball."

CATFISH HUNTER

As much as Jimmy "Catfish" Hunter was admired as a pitcher, he was even more respected as a person. At the end of his 15-year major league career he was basically the same quiet, unassuming fellow he had been when he signed a $75,000 contract with the Kansas City Athletics right out of Perquimans High School in Hertford, North Carolina. Here's a story that shows that Hunter never got a swelled head.

In 1986 in his second year on the ballot, Hunter received 289 votes in the Hall of Fame balloting, only 30 votes shy of election. His election the following year was a virtual certainty. Yet, after Jack Lang, the secretary of the Baseball Writers' Association of America and the well-known herald of the Hall of Fame voting results, called Hunter in January of 1987 to give him the good news, Jimmy hung up the phone, turned to his wife, Helen, and said, "Do you think that was the real Jack Lang?"

And how did Hunter pick up the nickname "Catfish"? Well, when the A's came to the Hunter farmhouse to sign the youngster to his first professional baseball contract, Hunter was down at the creek fishing. The team's representatives waited, and eventually Hunter came home, carrying a string of catfish he had pulled out of the creek. It's a nice story except that it isn't true. The whole thing was a complete fabrication by Charlie Finley, the owner of the A's, who wanted all his hot young prospects to have catchy nicknames to pique the public's interest in them.

Hunter went along with the ruse only to humor Finley, but as the years went by he found that the bogus nickname gave him a certain advantage. "None of my friends ever used that nickname," says Hunter. "I was always 'Jimmy' to my friends, so, whenever somebody in the stands at the ballpark would holler 'Catfish,' I never even turned around. I knew they didn't know me."

BRIAN KINGMAN

Even though Seattle Mariners pitcher Mike Moore won his final two starts of 1987, the last thing he expected to get was a congratulatory telegram, since he also lost a total of 19 games on the season.

But get one he did, from former Oakland A's hurler Brian Kingman, who complimented him on having the guts to risk losing 20 games: "A lot of guys bail out at 19 and don't pitch the last 10 days. You did. Congratulations!"

Kingman, the last major league pitcher to lose 20 games in one season by virtue of his 8–20 record in 1980, also joked that he was grateful that Moore "kept me from losing my identity in baseball trivia."

SANDY KOUFAX

Baseball history is full of stories about young pitchers with great speed but no control who never learn to harness the power in their arms. Left-handed fireballers in particular have been notorious for lacking control. The left-hander who over-came legendary wildness to become not only a Hall of Famer but also one of the game's most dominating players ever was Sandy Koufax.

Before becoming a professional baseball player, Koufax, a native of Brooklyn, New York, attended the University of Cincinnati on an athletic scholarship to play . . . basketball! As a forward on UC's freshman team, Koufax was a good rebounder and averaged 9.7 points per game.

UC's freshman basketball coach, Ed Jucker, happened to also be the school's varsity baseball coach. Jucker had no idea that Koufax was a baseball player, and Koufax asked for a try-out only after he learned that the baseball team would be making a spring trip to exotic New Orleans.

Because of the early-season cold weather, Koufax's tryout took place in a dimly lit field house under the grandstands of UC's football stadium. Koufax's blazing but erratic fastballs so terrified the team's veteran catcher that after three pitches he took off his mask and mitt, handed them to Jucker, and said, "Somebody else is going to have to catch that guy."

Years later, after Koufax had become the country's collective image of the virtually unhittable pitcher, Jucker liked to momentarily confound and then amuse audiences on the banquet circuit concerning the cause of Koufax's infamous early

wildness by claiming: "I'm the guy who converted Sandy Koufax into a left-hander!"

In the years from 1962 through 1966, Koufax won 14, 25, 19, 26, and 27 games and led the National League in ERA every one of those years. Despite his having been the game's most dominating pitcher during that time, Koufax was forced to retire at the age of 32 after the 1966 World Series because of circulation problems in his golden left arm. Because the Baltimore Orioles swept Koufax's Los Angeles Dodgers, Sandy was able to start only one game in the Series, the second. The Orioles' Davey Johnson, a pretty fair country hitter for a second baseman, singled off Koufax in the sixth inning of that second game, and as things turned out Johnson's single became the last hit ever surrendered by Koufax. For months afterward Johnson was unable to resist bragging about this accomplishment, until he repeated the boast in front of Koufax himself.

"I got the last hit you ever gave up," said Johnson proudly.

"Yeah, that's why I retired," countered Koufax.

TOMMY LASORDA

Len Matuszek, who played off and on in the majors from 1981 through 1987, finished up his career with the Los Angeles Dodgers. He remembers an incident involving outfielder Cesar Cedeno that would only make sense with former Dodgers manager Lasorda as one of the main characters.

"One Sunday in 1986 we're playing a one-o'clock game after having played the night before," says Matuszek. "Of course, ballplayers always hate a day game following a night game, and this day was no exception. Everybody's feeling kind of sluggish and unenthusiastic.

"Well, in the very first inning somebody gets hurt or gets sick, and Tommy decides he wants Cesar Cedeno to pinch-hit. He starts looking up and down the dugout bench for Cedeno, but he doesn't see him. That's because Cesar is back in the clubhouse, eating. He's not even dressed for the game. He's still in his sleeves, shorts, and sanitary socks.

"Lasorda sends Bill Russell, one of his coaches, to get Cedeno. Russell runs into the clubhouse and says to Cedeno, 'Tommy wants you to pinch-hit.'

"Cedeno, who's still stuffing his face, can't believe it. 'Whattaya mean, "pinch-hit"?' says Cedeno. 'It's only the first inning!'

"Russell goes back to the dugout and tells Tommy that Cedeno is not going to be able to hit, and he tells him why. Tommy is highly irritated, but he's forced to burn a left-handed pinch hitter, which he didn't want to do.

"Cedeno knows he's in the doghouse now, so after he's dressed he comes into the dugout and starts walking over to Tommy. He's got one hand behind his back and he's saying, '*Lo siento*, Tommy, *lo siento*—I'm sorry, I'm sorry—but here' . . . and he hands Lasorda the biggest sandwich you've ever seen, as a peace offering. I mean this sandwich was huge!

"Lasorda can't help but laugh, and later in the game he again calls on Cedeno to pinch-hit. This time Cesar goes up to bat, and he even gets a hit. And he says, 'See, that was too early before. You didn't need me then, Skip.'"

MICKEY MANTLE

The New York Yankees' Mickey Mantle was more than a
star, more than the best player on what was the best team
in baseball for much of the 1950s and '60s. For millions of
fans Mantle was an almost mythic hero, whose gifts of extraordinary speed and power were tragically diminished by
chronic injuries and alcoholism. As great a career as he had,
Mantle himself felt that he could have and should have done
better, much better, so that he would have been what many
felt he was destined to be: the greatest to ever play the game.

For a long time Mantle grossly underestimated how much
he meant to his millions of fans, even long after he had hung
up his spikes. Finally, with the outpouring of love and concern that he received from the public when he was dying of
liver cancer in 1995, Mantle began to understand the special
place he held in the hearts of so many.

Something Mantle never did fully comprehend was the
fanatical way people pursued his autograph. Of course,
Mickey was aware of the value of his signature—he made millions signing his name during the last couple of decades of
his life—but he never really understood why somebody would
treasure his autograph.

Mantle liked to poke fun at himself and the whole idea of
the autograph craze by telling the following joke: "When I
die, I'm going to be met at the Pearly Gates by St. Peter, who's
going to say, 'Sorry, Mick, you can't come in because of all
the bad things you did in life, but before you go, God wants
you to sign these baseballs.'"

DON
POLLARD

ROGER MARIS

It took a long time, but Roger Maris's single-season home-run record of 61 in 1961 was finally recognized as one of the greatest achievements in baseball history. Some fans resented Maris for having the effrontery to challenge the great Babe Ruth, who had hit 60 homers in 1927, and a controversy arose over the fact that Maris in 1961 was playing in a 162-game season, while the Babe had set his record in one of the old 154-game seasons. Since Maris needed the extra eight games to surpass Ruth, Commissioner Ford Frick ordered that both men be listed in the record books—Ruth as the holder of the home-run record for the shorter season, Maris as the holder of the record for the longer season. In recent years there has been talk about Maris's record being in imminent danger, but no contemporary slugger has really come close to breaking it.

Back in 1961 Roger Kahn, the famed author of *The Boys of Summer*, followed the last few weeks of Maris's Babe Ruth chase in order to write an article for a national sports publication. Here is what Kahn remembers about Maris and the media circus that developed around him.

"When the article began," says Kahn, "both Maris and Mantle had a shot at Ruth's record, so I went to cover both of them pursuing Ruth. Mantle dropped out—when he passed Gehrig at 48 he said to Roger, 'I've got my man'— and the press began to swarm around Roger. Eventually, there were 60 or 70 people covering him.

"I kept notes on the dumbest questions. Somebody said, 'Do you play around on the road?' Which was then unusable.

"Maris said, 'That's my business.'

"And the reporter, trying to get Maris to talk, said, 'I play around on the road.' Maris said, 'That's your business.'

"Somebody else said, 'Would you rather hit 60 home runs or bat .300?'

"And then in one game he had hit a breaking ball, and some green reporter asked, 'Was that ball breaking in on you?' Maris said, 'Well, seeing as how he's a right-handed pitcher and I'm a left-handed hitter, I'd say, "Yes."'

"And then there were little moments . . . Maris said something about 'the damn reporters,' and Elston Howard, sitting at the next locker, said, 'If I had 53 homers (or whatever it was at the time), I wouldn't be complaining about the reporters.'

"The sense was that Maris didn't want to be changed by this, and of course he couldn't avoid it. For instance, he couldn't go to a delicatessen in New York where he liked the sandwiches and be left alone. The experience was frightening to him. He said, 'They bust in on me even in church.' So that's the thrust of the piece: here's a man who's comfortable with being the typical ballplayer, but he's no longer a typical ballplayer.

"Maris never really blew up, and he wasn't as difficult as he's been depicted. There wasn't much of any publicity-department help around in those days to protect him, either, so Maris had to pretty much handle the press by himself. As trying as it must have been, he almost always talked to us reporters, although I do remember one night when he wouldn't come out to meet the press. I think he'd gone hitless in a doubleheader, and he sat in the trainer's room, which is always off-limits to the media, with his brother. A reporter said to the Yankees' manager, Ralph Houk, 'How can his brother be in there, and I can't?'

"And Houk said, 'You're telling me I can't let a man's god-damned brother talk to him?'

"Well, I did my story, and I never knew whether Maris read it or not until I ran into him the following spring training and he said, with great geniality and sincerity, 'Of all the horseshit that was written about me last year, yours was the best.'

"I guess you take literary criticism where you find it."

BILLY MARTIN

Although he had his moments, especially in the 1953 World Series when he won the MVP Award for batting .500, Billy Martin was not a great player. In a way, his playing career as a heady, super-aggressive second baseman was merely a training period for his real vocation as a major league manager.

Whenever Martin took over, a team immediately played better, smarter, and more aggressive baseball. A master of the rule book, a great teacher, and a keen motivator, Martin was, above all, the most intense of competitors, who would do anything to win a ball game. Billy was always looking for an edge, and he often found one . . . but not always.

As the manager of the New York Yankees, Martin made a strange move during a 3–2 loss to the Detroit Tigers on September 18, 1985, that Yankees fans are still trying to figure out.

With the score tied and two runners on base, the Yankees' left-handed-batting third baseman, Mike Pagliarulo, went up to bat against the Tigers' Mickey Mahler, a left-handed pitcher. Martin ordered Pagliarulo to bat right-handed. Now, it's true that "the book" dictates that ideally you pit a right-handed batter against a left-handed pitcher, but Pagliarulo had never before batted right-handed in his major league career. "Pags" did as he was ordered, and the rest of the Yankees watched in curious and confident anticipation.

Yankees designated hitter Don Baylor recalls, "I was sure it was a trick play. Billy's famous for trick plays."

"After strike one, I was thinking, 'OK, now comes the trick.' Nothing happened.

"After strike two, I figured, 'OK, here it comes.' Nothing.

"Then it was strike three, and I found out what the trick was: the trick was on us."

MASCOTS

A reporter once asked Ted Giannoulas, the Famous Chicken (formerly known as the San Diego Chicken), if he thought he'd ever be elected to the National Baseball Hall of Fame.

Giannoulas replied, "Who knows? They've got a broadcasters' wing, and they've got a writers' wing. Maybe one day they'll have a chicken wing."

Ever since Marge Schott became majority owner of the Cincinnati Reds, the city of Cincinnati has been embarrassed by her public fawning over her St. Bernard dogs, and Reds fans have resisted her repeated attempts to have them adopt "Schottzie" (and later, "Schottzie 02") as the team's mascot.

Oblivious to the public's snickering, Marge provided Schottzie an office at Riverfront Stadium, featured her in the Reds' media guide ahead of front-office executives, and produced a line of slow-moving Schottzie souvenirs. When Pete Rose was managing the Reds, he went along with the gag, even doing television commercials with Marge and the dog, but in truth he found all the fuss over Schottzie as galling as everybody else.

Author Roger Kahn and Rose were shooting the breeze one day in Rose's Riverfront Stadium office when Rose mentioned that he'd recently purchased a baby lion as a pet. Intrigued, Kahn asked, "What in the world are you going to do with a lion when it grows up?"

Without batting an eye, Rose replied, "Teach it to eat the dog."

After the Famous Chicken, the Phillie Phanatic is generally accounted the most entertaining mascot in the major leagues, but not everybody was amused by the Phanatic when Dave Raymond (now retired as a mascot) was the man inside the furry green "Big Bird–like" costume. Dodgers manager Tommy Lasorda, for one, thought the Phillie Phanatic as played by Raymond was downright obnoxious.

During a Dodgers-Phillies game in 1988, as a regular part of his routine the Phanatic beat up a dummy dressed in a Dodgers uniform. Lasorda stormed out of the Dodgers' dugout to object and began giving the Phanatic some of his own medicine. Raymond at first thought Lasorda was merely playing along with his routine but realized otherwise when Lasorda bashed him over the head with the dummy and tried to yank the Phanatic's head off. "OK, the gloves are off," said Raymond. Later in the same game he brought the Dodgers dummy out again and fed it a slice of pizza, an obvious insult directed toward Lasorda's weight problem.

Lasorda's feuding with the Phanatic came to a head in 1991 when the Dodgers visited Veterans Stadium shortly after the All-Star break. Before the final game of the series on

July 17, Lasorda eloquently aired his complaint: "I've worn three uniforms in my day, and I've been proud as a man can be of all three. I've worn the Boy Scout uniform, the uniform of the U.S. Army, and the Dodgers uniform, and I don't want to see some idiot making a spectacle of any of them.

"If he [the Phanatic] wants to entertain, wants to dance, wants to carry kids around, that's great. But I don't believe in demonstrating violence in the ballpark. And that's what he does with the dummy."

The Phanatic, who had hugged and kissed the Dodgers' dummy to the tune of "I Want to Hold Your Hand" during the previous day's game, withdrew his olive branch and re-declared war on Lasorda. In the seventh inning he ran his four-wheeler over a couple of plastic Dodgers helmets and several cans of Slim-Fast, the diet milk shake product endorsed by the Dodgers' manager. He then sped off past the Dodgers' dugout and stuck his long tongue out at Lasorda. Adding injury to insult, the Phillies swept the three-game series and extended the Dodgers' losing streak to seven games.

When Joe DiMaggio was in the midst of his famous 56-game hitting streak, his favorite bat was somehow stolen out of the Yankees' bat rack. The Yankees published an appeal for its return in the New York newspapers, and remarkably the bat was returned.

Although it wasn't as important as DiMaggio's bat, Seattle Mariners pitcher Chris Bosio helped retrieve another stolen baseball article: the head of a minor league team's mascot.

In July of 1996, Bosio was in Lancaster, California, rehabbing a bum right knee with Seattle's Single A California League entry. While being interviewed on a morning radio talk show, Bosio learned that Lancaster Jethawks officials and fans were upset that a week earlier someone had stolen the costumed head of the team's mascot, Kaboom. Bosio immediately spoke out on the air. "Bring back our head," he said.

Five hours later Kaboom's head was found alongside the road in nearby Bouquet Canyon. After the head was taken to the Jethawks' ballpark and cleaned up, Kaboom made a triumphant return while Bosio warmed up as the day's starting pitcher. After his successful four-inning stint, Bosio said, "I guess I do have a job after baseball—Bosio, P.I. I'll find missing mascots for all sports."

WILLIE MAYS

Although the essentials of baseball always remain the same, many things about the game have changed and changed dramatically over the years. A 1954 *Life* magazine article by Earl Brown about Willie Mays shows that there is a world of difference between the way ball clubs treat young players now and the way they treated them back then.

True, when he first arrived in New York in 1951, the 20-year-old Mays was probably unsophisticated, and he may have been a bit immature—the article depicts him as delighting in waking up his older roommate, Monte Irvin, by sticking a finger in Irvin's ear or by dousing him with a glass of cold water—but from our vantage point today it looks as if the the Giants saw fit to have a 61-year-old scout named Frank Forbes practically baby-sit him off the field. Engaging in a form of "protection" that even today's youngest major league players would consider to be an insulting and embarrassing invasion of privacy, Forbes tried to keep starry-eyed young females from distracting Mays by confiscating and tearing up the love notes and phone numbers they would attempt to slip Willie outside the Giants' clubhouse. And when he felt that they were called for, Forbes was ready to resort to stronger measures, too.

According to the article, Forbes was relaxing one day in a Harlem bar when somebody came in and said that a certain woman, well known around the neighborhood, was in the drugstore down the street having a soda. At first, Forbes and his companion laughed at this bit of incongruous news because they knew that straight whiskey was this experienced woman's beverage of choice. Then, with a sinking feeling Forbes realized that the drugstore was Mays's favorite hangout. The old scout rushed out of the bar, down the street, and into the drugstore, where he found the woman sitting at the counter next to Willie and chatting quietly. Forbes sat down beside the woman and ordered a double chocolate ice-cream soda with extra whipped-cream topping. When it came, he intentionally knocked the entire thing into the woman's lap (while pretending to be reaching for a straw) and then, pretending to try to catch the glass before it fell off the counter, knocked the woman completely off her stool and onto the floor, effectively defeating her attempt to get close to Mays. Forbes apologized profusely but didn't regret his actions. "When she hit the floor she was really a mess," said Forbes, "but I had to do it to protect Willie."

If you wish to retain unsullied your memories or image of the young Willie Mays as the personification of innocent, joyful exuberance on the diamond, you should stop reading now.

Mays surely did love to play the game, but he was also more sophisticated and conscious of the benefits of an engaging image than yesterday's sportswriters imagined.

The writers made the way "the Say Hey Kid's" cap flew off when he ran an endearing part of the Mays legend, but Willie revealed in 1991 that it was an intentional gimmick calculated to make him a more colorful performer.

"I started wearing a cap that was too big for me," said Mays. "And sure enough, every time I ran from first to second and wheeled to my left, that cap would simply fly off just as if I'd been running so fast I'd run out from under it. The cap would fly off when I stole a base, and so after dusting myself off I'd have to go back and pick it up. The moment's delay would keep the fans worked up."

Willie was fast, but give him extra credit for knowing that illusion can be more powerful than reality.

Believe it or not, when the Giants moved from New York to San Francisco after the 1957 season, Willie Mays was not universally welcomed with open arms by Bay Area baseball fans. Some San Franciscans felt that Mays was too much of a New York hero, while others feared that the hoopla surrounding Mays would diminish the reputation of Joe DiMaggio, who had done wondrous things for the Triple A San Francisco Seals of the old Pacific Coast League before becoming a great star for the New York Yankees.

Foremost among the latter was Lefty O'Doul, a beloved native San Franciscan who, in addition to being a former National League batting champion, had been DiMaggio's manager on the Seals back in the mid-1930s. O'Doul never had anything complimentary to say about Mays, but the following story by writer Charles Einstein shows that when O'Doul was being honest he was just as impressed with Mays as everybody else.

"I remember being at Candlestick Park on a real cold night," says Einstein. "It's the last of the seventh, and with the Giants way ahead everyone's starting to leave. O'Doul is all bundled up and sitting in one of the boxes in the mezzanine. Somebody says, 'Why don't we get out of here, Lefty?'

"And Lefty says, 'Alright.' But when he gets to the door, he turns around and says, 'Wait a minute. Lemme watch Mays hit.'

"O'Doul stayed to watch Mays hit, and then he left."

THE METS OF 1986

When the 1986 New York Mets found themselves trailing in the late innings, the members of their "Rally Cap Club" didn't just sit in the dugout reading their fan mail. They tried to turn the score around by turning their ball caps inside out, a routine they borrowed from the college ranks. The stunt must have been magic, because the Mets went all the way in 1986, winning the National League Championship Series against the Houston Astros and the World Series against the Boston Red Sox in some of the most exciting postseason games in baseball history.

Moreover, although it's not well known, an innovative variation of the Rally Cap routine helped the Mets win the wild and critical sixth World Series game made famous by Red Sox first baseman Bill Buckner's infamous error on Mookie Wilson's slow, twisty roller. With the Mets down by two runs, utility man Danny Heep and pitchers Roger McDowell, Bob Ojeda, Jesse Orosco, and Ron Darling watched the bottom of the 10th inning in the office of Charlie Samuels, the Mets' equipment manager.

Spying Samuels's collection of football helmets that decorated his office, the desperate Mets cheerleaders were inspired to have a helmet rally. Donning Miami Dolphins, Chicago Bears, New England Patriots, Tampa Bay Buccaneers, and Iowa Hawkeyes helmets, McDowell and cronies did head butts every time the Mets scored a run and obviously were instrumental in bringing about the two-out, three-run outburst that gave them a most exciting and unlikely victory.

The Rally Cap and Rally Helmet magic may have helped the Mets win the 1986 World Series, but, on the other hand, the Mets were cursed at the conclusion of the Series because of the despicable action of one idiotic Mets fan. Long after the Mets had won the seventh game of the Series, the dejected Red Sox players and Jack Rogers, Boston's traveling secretary, were walking across the Shea Stadium diamond toward the team bus when the aforementioned idiot threw a beer bottle that hit Rogers in the head and knocked him to the ground, bleeding and unconscious. Even more outrageous, according to Roger Clemens in his autobiography, *Rocket Man,* was the behavior of two New York City policemen, who "stood there laughing at him." At that moment the baseball gods turned their backs on the Mets and ordained that they should suffer decades of futility.

Mets fans who scoff at the Jack Rogers Curse should ask Red Sox fans about the Curse of the Bambino, which fell upon the Red Sox back in 1920 when Boston owner Harry Frazee sold Babe Ruth to the Yankees. Any Red Sox fan can tell you that the team has not won the World Series since.

THE MINOR LEAGUES

Left-hander Dan Neville was an outstanding minor league pitcher and major league prospect who led the Florida State League in ERA (1.94) in 1961. In 1964 he won 14 games for the San Diego Padres of the Pacific Coast League, and the Cincinnati Reds called him up to the big leagues at the end of that season. Although Neville warmed up in earnest in the Reds' bullpen, he never actually entered a major league game; shortly thereafter, a sore arm ended his promising career.

Neville now has fun sharing stories about his minor league escapades with the regulars at Crosley's, the best sports bar in Cincinnati. Here are a few of his best stories.

"I played with a number of guys in the minors who went on to become stars or at least solid players in the majors: Johnny Bench, Pete Rose, Tony Perez, Lee May, Tommy Helms, Mel Queen, and Art Shamsky. I remember one spring training game in 1964 when Tommy Helms and I were with the Reds' major league squad in Palm Beach, Florida, for a game against the Milwaukee Braves. Helms was named National League Rookie of the Year in 1966 and went on to become an All-Star second baseman and Gold Glove winner for the Reds, but that was later. At this point Tommy was still basically a bush leaguer. Anyway, Tommy and I were sitting on the bench, paying attention to the game and to everything Reds manager Freddie Hutchinson said or did, just hoping like hell to get a chance to get into the game, when Hutchinson said, 'Helms . . . grab a bat.'

"Well, Tommy was excited as all get-out, thinking he was being called on to pinch-hit. He jumped off the bench, started twisting around to get loosened up, and reached for a bat in the bat rack. But before he could even touch it, Hutchinson lifted up his leg and said, 'Come here and knock the dirt out of my spikes.'"

"I met a lot of crazy guys in the minors. We were all young and foolish, really. One guy I'll never forget was Tommy Tischinski, a catcher who made it up to the majors for three seasons with Minnesota. When Tommy and I were playing for the Reds' farm team in Macon, Georgia, Tommy had a girlfriend he really liked who lived in Tampa, Florida. Every other day Tommy would jump in his car and drive to Tampa to see her. It would take him three hours to get there, and it's a five-hour drive. One day I asked him how he made a five-hour trip in three hours. Tommy said, 'I just get on the expressway and drive 120 or 130 miles per hour.'

"'Don't the cops stop you?' I asked.

"'Hell, no,' he said. 'They see somebody going that fast, they figure he's crazy, and they don't want to mess with him.'"

"Back in the sixties drinking was a big part of baseball, and I certainly did my share. One time when I was playing Triple A ball in San Diego, Ted Davidson, another pitcher, and I went to some television benefit for disadvantaged kids in the morning. Two San Diego Chargers football players were there too, and after the show we went over to the restaurant that one of those two Chargers owned for lunch and some beers. Well, we wound up staying all afternoon and got pretty plastered. When we got to the ballpark, I went up to the bulletin board in the clubhouse to see what I was scheduled to do that day. I was squinting up at the bulletin board, trying to focus my eyes, and I was kind of weaving back and forth.

Dave Bristol, our manager, came by and saw me there and said, 'What's the matter with you?'

"'I'm drunk,' I said.

"'Drunk? Then you ain't putting on a uniform.'

"'Why not?' I said. 'I ain't pitching tonight. What difference does it make?' Bristol started getting mad then, so I ratted on Davidson. 'I ain't the only one who's drunk, you know. Davidson's drunk too.'

"And of course, I didn't listen to Bristol. I got dressed and went out on the field for BP. Bristol and the San Diego general manager saw me staggering around in the outfield—it's a wonder I didn't get beaned in the head with a fly ball—so the GM called me and Davidson into his office. He said, 'You're both suspended for three days.'

"Now I got mad. I went home to my apartment and told my wife, Rosemarie, to start packing because I was quitting the team and we were leaving town. Before long the GM called and said to report back to the ballpark while the Reds considered the situation. Davidson and I sat up in the stands in our civilian clothes—Rosemarie was still at home packing—and in the middle of the game the GM came up to us and said, 'The suspension is lifted.'

"Davidson and I were so happy we went down to Tijuana after the game to celebrate and stayed out till four in the morning getting drunk again!

"I got home, and there was Rosemarie waiting for me, with everything we owned packed and ready to go.

"'Unpack,' I said. 'We're staying.' Boy, was she mad!"

"Another time during spring training we had an off-day at the Reds' camp in Tampa, so I drove over to Orlando, where the Minnesota Twins trained, to visit one of their players, an old friend of mine named Gary Dotter. Gary, Jim Merritt, Ken Retzer, and I got drunk in Gary's hotel room. At some point we started talking about this huge fountain out in the middle of this big man-made lake we could see right outside the hotel window. Well, Retzer bet me $50 I couldn't swim out to the fountain and back. I didn't much like Retzer, and he didn't like me. Hell, that's why he bet me $50 I couldn't swim out to the fountain and back—he wanted to see me drown!

"I didn't want to do it at first because I didn't have a bathing suit, but Retzer said he had one and gave it to me to put on. It was red with a big white heart on it. It was actually a pair of underwear, but I didn't notice. That's how drunk I was. I must have been a sight walking through the hotel lobby in that damn thing.

"So I dove into the lake and swam and swam and swam and got right up to the fountain. But I couldn't get all the way to it, because the spray coming off it was so powerful it kept knocking me backward. I didn't have any choice but to turn around and swim back to the shore. I was pretty exhausted by that time, and before I got halfway back I just completely ran out of gas. I started swallowing water, and I was screaming for help: 'Help! Help me! I'm drowning!'

"Merritt was on the shore, hollering, 'Come on, Dan; you can make it. You can make it!'

"Swimming was out of the question, and pretty soon I couldn't even tread water. I thought, 'I'm going to die.' I was resigned to it, so I finally relaxed and straightened my body to begin sinking.

"Then my feet hit bottom, and I stood up in water that only came up a little above my waist.

"When I walked out of the lake, Merritt and Dotter were laughing so hard they couldn't stand up straight.

"Even though I didn't swim all the way back, Retzer paid me the $50. And my manager at Tampa, Dave Bristol again, found out about it from the Minnesota scouts. I know that because the next day I was lacing up my spikes in the club-house when he walked by and said, 'Enjoy your little swim?'"

Chalk it up to cultural differences or to something more personal, but some minor league ballplayers seem destined never to make it out of the bush leagues.

Take the case of Latin infielder Fabio Gomez, who despite an undistinguished career on the diamond remains something of a legend in the farm system of the Cleveland Indians.

While playing for the Burlington (NC) Indians in 1987, Gomez decided he wanted to buy a television set to send as a present to his mother back home. Coach Roger Hill took Gomez to a local appliance store, then to a department store, to a furniture store, and to another appliance store. None of the TVs in any of the stores satisfied Gomez. Finally, at a fifth store Hill said, "Fabio, we've looked at a lot of TVs. They all look pretty good to me. What in the world is wrong with all these TVs you keep passing up?"

"They no speak español," said Gomez.

A few years later Gomez received a bad break he should have been able to avoid. Gomez had a sore hand and went to see a witch doctor, seeking relief from the pain. The witch doctor diagnosed "evil spirits" and, attempting to drive them out, broke Gomez's hand with a hammer.

Let them into a game free and baseball fans will do nearly anything you ask of them, even stifle their habit of littering the grandstands, as old a baseball tradition as booing the umpires. That's what happened at Kingsport, Tennessee's, J. Fred Johnson Stadium during a Friday-night doubleheader on August 16, 1991, between the Appalachian League Bluefield Orioles and the Kingsport Mets.

Two thousand fans were admitted to the game for the price of one recyclable item and a promise to pick up after themselves at the end of the night. During the fifth inning of each game containers were passed down each row, and altogether the environmentally friendly fans deposited 340 pounds of newspaper, 450 pounds of cardboard, and 220 pounds of various other recyclable materials. With maintenance crews enjoying the night off, the fans upheld their end of the bargain and left the stadium completely free of trash.

When prematurely retired basketball superstar Michael Jordan decided he wanted to play professional baseball, many observers doubted that he would ever make the major leagues. Skeptics cited his late start and his lack of experience—Jordan hadn't played baseball since high school. *Sports Illustrated* went so far as to say that Jordan shouldn't have even gotten a chance to try because his playing on a minor league team would deprive some deserving youngster with a more realistic shot at making the majors of a roster spot.

None of this mattered in the least to minor league baseball fans. The Chicago White Sox announced on February 7, 1994, that they had signed Jordan to a minor league contract, and in the next four and a half days the White Sox's Triple A affiliate, the Nashville Sounds, sold $200,000 worth of tickets . . . with no assurance that Jordan would even play for the Sounds during the 1994 season.

As it turned out, Jordan was assigned to Chicago's Double A affiliate in the Southern League, the Birmingham Barons. Despite Jordan's mediocre performance (.202, 3 homers, 51 RBI), the Barons set a franchise record for home attendance (467,867) and drew 518,328 customers on the road, accounting for 38.7 percent of all Southern League attendance for the year.

After pitching for the Detroit Tigers in 1968, Jon Warden hurt his arm during the following spring training and spent 1969 pitching in the minor leagues for the Omaha Royals of the Triple A American Association. That Omaha team was stocked with former major leaguers, including one Bill Faul, a short, right-handed pitcher who'd had cups of coffee with the Tigers, Cubs, and Giants.

"Faul was a little guy who was built like a fireplug," says Warden, "but, boy, did he have an arm. He could really throw.

"Our manager that year was Jack McKeon. Jack was a funny guy and a great guy to play for, but for some reason Faul hated him, just couldn't stand him.

"We had a 17-game road trip that year because they were playing the College World Series in Omaha. This was before they started regional tournaments. They brought all the teams in and played the whole thing in Omaha over a two-week period.

"We were boarding the bus that would take us to the airport for the start of this long road trip. Although he'd put his suitcase on the bus, Faul wasn't on the bus yet. Dave Nicholson, a big, free-swinging outfielder, took Faul's suitcase down out of the overhead luggage rack and said, 'Let's see what Bill's taking on the road trip with him.'

"Nicholson was curious because we thought Faul was kind of a weirdo. Bill hypnotized himself before games, and he never wanted to take a shower. He said that too much water was bad for the body, that your natural oils would cleanse your skin.

"So Nicholson opened Faul's suitcase, and what we saw inside was one pair of pants, one shirt, one pair of underwear, a shaving kit—for a 17-game road trip, mind you—and a .357 Magnum in a holster with a box of shells. That's what he packed for 17 days. Everyone went, 'Holy smoke!' Nicholson closed the suitcase, and off we went.

"We played a series in Tulsa and then went into Des Moines, where it had been raining. One of our pitchers, Chris Zachary, had gone out with this real pretty girl in Tulsa, and Faul decided he wanted to date her too. He told Zachary, 'Hey, man, that chick was out of sight. If you give me her phone number, I'll do anything.'

"Zachary said, 'You'll do anything?'

"Faul said, 'Yeah, yeah. I'll do anything.'

"Zachary looked down and saw a toad jumping around. He bent down, picked it up, and said, 'How about eating this toad?'

"Faul frowned and sighed but then said, 'Yeah, I'll do it.'

"Faul wanted the toad washed off first before he ate it, so we got a paper cup, filled it with water out of a mud hole, and put the toad in to wash it off. Faul took the toad, gathered himself for a couple of seconds, then said, 'OK, here we go.' He popped the whole toad into his mouth and started chewing. He was making these crunching sounds just as if he were eating a mouthful of Doritos. Crunch, crunch, crunch, crunch. He swallowed the whole thing and turned to Zachary with an expectant look on his face.

"Zachary said, 'Ah, I've changed my mind. I'm not going to give you her number.'

"That really got Faul ticked off. 'You son of a bitch,' he hollered. 'You promised!'

"Zachary said, 'You've got to do better than that. You've got to top that.'

"Faul said, 'No way. You promised! A deal's a deal.'

"But Zachary wouldn't give him the number. They argued a little longer, and then Zachary said, 'We're going to Indianapolis in two days, and you've got to eat something over there. You've got to eat a mouse.'

" 'No, I'm not eating a mouse,' Faul said. 'No way. I'm not going to do that.'

" 'Fine,' said Zachary. 'No mouse, no phone number.'

"Well, Faul wanted that girl's phone number now worse than before, so after we got settled in Indianapolis, Zachary and I went out shopping for Faul. And we took Faul along with us. I said, 'Look, Bill, what do you want to eat tonight? The guys are all expecting some big deal. We've got to get something. What's it gonna be?' We went into one pet store, but all the animals were too big.

"So we went to a Walgreens, and back then every Walgreens had little pets for sale. I saw a tank of goldfish, so, I said, 'OK, Bill, how about a goldfish?'

"Faul said, 'Ah, anybody can eat a goldfish.'

'Maybe so,' I told him, 'but let's buy three of them just in case.'

"We left Walgreens and moved on to another place which had some little white mice. Right away Bill started saying, 'Nope, nope, no way. I ain't eating a mouse.'

"'OK, fine. Let's just get one for the hell of it,' I said. So I bought one, and we took it out of the store in a little paper carton, like the kind you get Chinese food in.

"The next place we hit had parakeets, and I immediately said to myself, 'Bingo!'

"'Bill, how about biting the head off a parakeet?' I said.

"'Oh, yeah, I'll do that,' he said.

"'Now, you've got to chew on it some too,' I said.

"'Yeah, yeah. No problem,' Faul said.

"I told the clerk we wanted to buy a parakeet, so she asked which one we wanted. There were about 15 blue ones and one green one. Faul said, 'I'll take the green one.' The clerk told Bill he could get the bird himself, so he reached into the cage to get the green parakeet; well, it pecked him on the hand. And I'm telling you that Faul's eyes widened and he looked as crazy and as bloodthirsty as a werewolf.

"The girl said, 'Do you want any corn or feed to go with your parakeet?'

"Bill said, 'This bird won't be alive long enough to eat any food.'

"The girl kind of backed away and had a look on her face as if to say, 'Whoa! What's the matter with this guy?'

"We took the parakeet out of the store in another chow mein box. So now we had a parakeet, a mouse, and three goldfish. I said, 'Alright! We're ready to go play some ball now!'

"We got to the ballpark, and Faul said, 'I'm not eating that mouse, I'm telling ya.'

"I said, 'OK, just bite the head off the parakeet, and that'll be good enough.'

"When it was time, Faul sat down on the trainer's table in the middle of the room, and everybody sort of gathered around. Catcher Jim Campanis, whose dad was the Dodgers' GM for years, turned on a tape recorder and started announcing the event: 'Here we are, ladies and gentlemen, in Indianapolis, Indiana, where Bill Faul is about to bite the head off a live parakeet.'

"Bill started breathing heavy, psyching himself up, and then he reached into the paper carton for the bird. As he pulled it out, the damn parakeet pecked him again. Bill's eyes widened just like before, and then he did it. Whomp! He bit the head right off that parakeet, and blood spurted all over the place. It sounds gross and disgusting, but it was one hell of a funny thing to see.

"Faul chewed away for about 30 seconds and then spit the head out. Somebody said, 'Hey, you didn't eat any of the body.' So Faul started gnawing on the rest of the bird, and pretty soon he had feathers stuck to his lips.

"McKeon came in and said, 'Everybody out. Everybody out of here.'

"I said, 'Skip, you want everybody out?'

" 'Yeah, I want everybody out.'

"I had a pistol that shot blanks in my locker, and I'd put a tear gas capsule in the gun. I shot the gun into the air vent, and within seconds the fans were blowing tear gas all over the locker room. That got everybody out of there in a hurry. When we were all assembled in the dugout, McKeon said, 'Look, you guys have got to stop messing with Faul. He's too dangerous. He's liable to kill somebody. You guys have got to leave him alone—especially you, Warden.'

"I said, 'Me? How come I always get blamed for everything? What did I do?'

" 'You probably bought him the damn parakeet!'

" 'Well, yes, I guess I did.'

"Of course, I didn't listen to McKeon. Back in the clubhouse I took the mouse and put it in Faul's pants pocket. I told everybody what I'd done; so after the game we were all watching Faul when he was changing at his locker. At that point, he was all unwound and feeling kind of embarrassed about what had happened. He slipped his trousers on—remember he was traveling with only two pair—and right away he felt the mouse jumping up and down in his pocket. It startled him, and he let out a scream. Then he took off the pants, laid them on a bench, took a bat out of the bat rack, smashed the mouse while it was still in his pocket, put the pants back on, and walked out.

"The next day I went over to Bill's room at the hotel. He was rooming alone because his roommate, Fran Healy, had gone to McKeon and said, 'I can't room with this guy. He sleeps with that .357 under his pillow, and in the afternoons he sits in the window of our room, pointing the gun at people walking by in the street, and saying, "Boom, could have had ya. Boom, could have had ya."'

"I banged on Faul's door, and he growled, 'Who is it?'

"'Jack McKeon,' I said, imitating McKeon's voice.

"The door opened up as far as the latch would let it, and the barrel of that .357 came through the opening. 'What the hell do you want?' said Faul.

"I almost had a heart attack. 'It's me, Bill! It's Warden!' I stammered.

"'Don't ever do that again,' Faul said. 'I could shoot that son of a bitch.'

"Believe me, I didn't do that again, and as a matter of fact, I finally took McKeon's advice and pretty much quit egging Faul on altogether."

KEVIN MITCHELL

During the 1993 All-Star break, Cincinnati Reds outfielder Kevin Mitchell flew home to San Diego to enjoy the three off-days with his family. For his return trip to Cincinnati, Mitchell scheduled the latest possible flight out of San Diego and then missed that flight.

Upset at Mitchell's cavalier attitude concerning his tardiness in reporting for work, Reds manager Davey Johnson called Mitchell into his office for a lecture. One thing led to another, and the meeting ended with Mitchell's taking a swing at his manager.

The fracas was the talk of the town, and that night the press-box statistician Gary Schatz told his wife about the incident. Schatz's three-year-old daughter, Holly, also listened to her daddy's story and offered an explanation for the conflict: "Maybe they don't have a Barney," she said, referring to her stuffed purple dinosaur that represents the children's pacifist TV character.

The next day when Schatz got ready to go to work, Holly said, "Daddy, don't forget Barney."

Schatz, who had completely forgotten her remark from the previous night, said, "What do I need Barney for?"

Holly replied, "You know, for the two children who can't play together without fighting, Kevin and Mitchell."

Holly didn't let Schatz leave the house until he packed her Barney along with his laptop computer and score books for the trip to the ballpark.

During the 1994 season Mitchell nearly beheaded Florida Marlins pitcher Chris Hammond with a vicious line drive hit right through the box. Hammond, a former teammate of Mitchell's on the Reds, avoided the missile at the last second and thus escaped injury; nevertheless, Chris was surely touched by the concern for his safety reflected in Mitchell's postgame comments about the play:

"That ball I hit scared the heck out of me. It was going right at his head. I said, 'What the heck are you doing? Duck, fool! Don't be getting my blood pressure up. I don't need a murder charge. I don't need a 187, killing a guy on the field. You're supposed to be a friend of mine. I don't need no murder charge.'"

DON MOSSI

Don Mossi is one of those players that fans of the baby boomer generation remember most fondly. Mossi was a pretty good left-handed pitcher who compiled a 101–80 lifetime record over 12 seasons, mostly with the Cleveland Indians and Detroit Tigers, but it wasn't his record that endeared him to us. It was his face. An angular face made unforgettable by bushy eyebrows, a perpetual five-o'clock shadow, and a pair of ears that seemed attached to the sides of his head like the handles of a loving cup trophy.

Although Mossi had no Cincinnati connection, he became in the mid-1970s the focal point of a huge, long-running Cincinnati Hot Stove League baseball party hosted by two Cincinnati Reds front-office employees, Tom Jackson and Doug Bureman. Here is Jackson's account of how Mossi's cult status in Cincinnati came about.

"The whole thing started in November of 1974. Doug and I were young bachelors in our late twenties at the time, and we tried to party every chance we got. We were sitting around one day looking at some baseball cards that were on the coffee table, and a card of Don Mossi just stood out from all the rest. We saw that his birthday is January 11, so we figured why not have a birthday party on that day in Don's honor? It turned out that the coming January 11 fell on a Saturday, so it worked out perfectly.

"We had the party at Doug's split-level town house, and about 80 people showed up. Some of the girls made a cake that accentuated Don's most prominent facial features, his ears, and at the height of the evening's festivities we called Don at his home in Ukiah, California, to wish him happy birthday. At first he didn't believe we were having a party in his honor, but we told him it was for real. It turned out to be a pretty crazy party, and it just took off from there. We wound up having our Don Mossi party for 12 straight years, and from the second year on we moved the party to a rental hall. The attendance peaked at over 450 people a year, two years in a row.

"The whole thing got to be pretty elaborate. We printed up admission tickets, made up T-shirts that we sold at cost— one showed Don in a cowboy outfit and said, 'Mossi's Posse'— and one year we even had a Don Mossi ice sculpture. We charged people three or four bucks to get in to help pay for the 'all-you-can-drink' beer we served, and each year the highlight of the evening was the long-distance phone call to Don. We gave out door prizes, and the best prize, which three people won each year, was the privilege of talking to Don for one minute.

"The party started out mocking Mossi, but as it went on year after year he became a hero, sort of a folk hero. We found out that he is a very decent guy, a real dedicated family man. Eleven out of the 12 years we called him to wish him happy birthday, he was at home, just sitting around the house with his wife and two daughters. He's never been to another major league baseball game since he retired, even though he lives only a hundred miles north of San Francisco. He likes to hunt and fish, and he works as a supervisor in a Masonite factory. Don's also a very, very quiet guy. He never says much at all. I actually visited him at his house in 1979. In the 20-minute conversation I had with him, I must have done all the talking for 18 minutes, and I'm a terrible conversationalist.

"In Don we picked the perfect guy for our party without knowing it beforehand. A lot of guys would have gotten mad and blown us off, but to Don it was no big deal. He even sent us stuff for our Don Mossi Museum, which was on display at the party each year. He sent us game-worn caps from all four major league teams he played for, some Don Mossi photos, an autographed baseball, and an instructional pitching film he 'starred in.' The film was woefully outdated—it just showed Don throwing off a mound for five minutes or so—but we showed it each year, and people went wild. Since we worked in baseball, we were able to obtain some legitimate Don Mossi items ourselves from the Indians and Tigers, but we also had some gag items in the Mossi Museum: Don's World Series ring—a cigar band—and his scrapbook, which was completely empty.

"One Don Mossi occurrence I'll never forget involved a guy named Brian Hunterman, who came to Cincinnati in 1979 to work for the Reds. Brian had no previous contact with any of us nor any previous clue about the party, yet when someone told him about the party and asked him if he wanted to go, he reached into his back pocket for his wallet and then pulled a Don Mossi baseball card out of it—proving that Don was a legend independent of our party. Needless to say, Brian became a regular at the parties.

"The twelfth party was our last. It was a heck of a lot of work to put on, and we got a little tired of it. We rationalized that it was appropriate to stop after 12 years because 12 years was the length of Don's major league career. We had wanted to fly Don in for an appearance at a party, but we could never convince him to come. He was just too modest to do it. Our only regret was that Don never came to Cincinnati to meet his adoring public. Other than that, our Don Mossi parties were nothing but a whole lot of laughs."

THURMAN MUNSON

Currently the director of public relations for the Topps Company, Marty Appel used to work as the public relations director for the New York Yankees. In that latter capacity, Appel was once taught a valuable lesson about baseball statistics by Thurman Munson, the hard-nosed, fiercely proud Yankees catcher who died in a tragic airplane crash in 1979.

"This started one day in the early 1970s," says Appel, "when the players were sitting around the clubhouse after batting practice. Thurman was reading the day's press notes, which as the team's PR director it was my job to write up and distribute to the members of the media. Press notes are mostly statistics (updated daily), but I'd also include all sorts of tidbits, such as notes about Yankees players who were among the league leaders in various categories. Once a month or so *The Sporting News* would publish fielding stats, and their latest issue showed that Thurman was second in the league in assists among catchers, with 25. Carlton Fisk of the Boston Red Sox was leading the league with 27. Well, I had put this information in my press notes for that day, and Thurman saw it. The problem was that Thurman couldn't stand Fisk, and he was so competitive he hated the idea that anybody would think Fisk was better than him.

"As I was walking through the clubhouse, Thurman waved me over to his locker.

"'What's the idea of showing me up like this?' he said, pointing to the press notes.

"'What are you talking about?' I said.

" 'This bullshit about me being behind Fisk in assists. Do you think for one minute he's got a better arm than me? I can't believe you'd use this! What a stupid statistic!' Thurman was really mad about it, and he finished his little tirade by saying, 'I'll show you.'

"A short while later the game got under way, and I was sitting up in the press box in my usual location. When our pitcher struck out his first batter of the game, Thurman dropped the ball, but he picked it up and snapped a throw down to first. I didn't look down at Thurman, but I immediately realized what the play meant: a putout for the first baseman and an assist for Thurman. In the next inning a second batter struck out, and again Thurman dropped the ball, picked it up, and threw to first to record the out. This time I did look down at home plate, and there was Thurman looking right back at me. He held up two fingers, as if to say, 'That's two assists.' A third guy struck out, and Thurman did it all one more time, earning his third assist of the game to put him one ahead of Fisk. This time when I looked down and saw Thurman looking up, he had a big grin on his face.

"After the game I said to him, 'I can't believe you did that.' He said, 'Did what?' He never would admit he dropped those third strikes on purpose, but he definitely made his point about catchers' assists."

HIDEO NOMO

Hideo Nomo, the Japanese pitcher with the windup that is the envy of contortionists everywhere, made a sensational debut in stateside major league baseball in 1995. Pitching for the Los Angeles Dodgers, Nomo baffled National League batters so thoroughly that not only was he a shoo-in to make the senior circuit's All-Star squad, but he was also named as the NL's starting pitcher. The Japanese media, which had closely followed en masse Nomo's adventures in America from the beginning of the season, almost got a little too close to their national hero prior to the playing of the 1995 All-Star Game.

While Nomo readied himself at his cubicle in the visitors' clubhouse at The Ballpark, in Arlington, Texas, a couple of dozen Japanese reporters studied his every move. When Nomo stood up and walked out of the room, the reporters rushed after him. They reappeared moments later, grinning sheepishly. All two dozen had followed him into the bathroom.

BOB OJEDA

It's common for major leaguers to save baseballs associated with special moments and achievements in their careers. It took Dodgers pitcher Bob Ojeda more than a decade to hit his first major league home run, so when it came in 1992 against the Expos in Montreal, Ojeda naturally wanted the ball for his trophy case.

Ojeda learned that the Expos fan who had corralled his home-run ball was willing to surrender it, for a price: three autographed baseballs.

"OK, it's a deal," said Ojeda, who started to look for a pen until he was informed that the fan wanted three *Orel Hershiser* autographed baseballs.

JUNIOR ORTIZ

Ex–Cleveland Indians pitcher Tommy Kramer remembers Indians catcher Junior Ortiz as a "real character" who had one unusual pet peeve.

"One thing Junior absolutely hated," says Kramer, "was the meetings we'd have for all the pitchers and catchers. Every team in the majors has these meetings so that everybody knows how to pitch the hitters on the other team, and you always have the meeting right before the start of each new series. Well, Junior just hated these meetings, thought they were a waste of time. He'd say, 'Dunno why we have these meetings. Same thing every time: Haaaaard inside, breaking balls away. Next hitter: Haaaaard inside, breaking balls away!'

"The pitching coach, Rich Adair, tried to tell him, 'Junior, some guys are different.' But Junior wasn't buying it.

"Well, one time we went into Toronto for a series against the Blue Jays. It's the first game of the series, so we have a pitchers-catchers meeting scheduled for 5:00. In some cities we'd meet in the locker room; in other cities we'd meet in a special meeting room or some place like that. In Toronto we met in the same room where we ate. There were a couple of tables in the room with tablecloths on them and chairs all around the tables.

"Guys start coming into the room one by one, and after a few minutes everybody's there except Junior. Rich Adair says, 'Has anybody seen Junior?' No, nobody's seen him lately. We wait a few minutes for Junior and then wait a few more minutes for him. Finally, Rich figures Junior's not coming, and he says, 'OK, I guess we'd better get the meeting started. All right, the Blue Jays lead off with Rickey Henderson, the left-field—'

"And from under the table comes this loud voice with a Spanish accent: 'Haaaaard inside, breaking balls away!'"

AMOS OTIS

Former Kansas City Royals relief ace Dan Quisenberry remembers outfielder Amos Otis as one of the most exceptional individuals he ever encountered in professional baseball.

"A.O., as we called him, was a great defensive centerfielder. He never missed the cutoff man, and we threw out a lot of runners at home because A.O. got the relay started right. He was such a great positioner and knew the tendencies of the hitters around the league so well that our manager, Whitey Herzog, would ask him, 'Where you going to play this guy, A.O.?'

"He was such a fluid runner that we never knew what gear he was in . . . first, second, or overdrive. A.O. also liked to steal bases standing up. He kept track of them and laughed like hell whenever he got one.

"A.O. called himself 'the Captain.' He wasn't the team's captain, but he liked for us to call him that, so we did.

"Sometimes he'd get moody, and to keep everybody away from him he'd put tape on the floor around his locker.

"A.O. was basically a very quiet guy, but when he had something to say, he said it. For instance, in my rookie year, 1979, we had just finished our last game prior to the three-day break for the All-Star Game. The Royals' owner, Ewing Kauffman, came into the clubhouse and started passing out envelopes of money. 'I want you boys to relax and have a good time during the break,' he said. 'Take your wife out to dinner on me.'

"Everybody was just accepting the envelopes, not even looking at them, and saying thanks, but A.O. said in a loud voice, 'If it's less than $100, keep it.' That was A.O., not afraid to say what he thought, to anybody. And by the way, each envelope contained exactly $100."

GAYLORD PERRY

Back in 1974 Gaylord Perry published an autobiography called *Me and the Spitter* in which he confessed to having applied every foreign substance to "the old apple but salt and pepper and chocolate sauce toppin'." The book made Gaylord some money and no doubt helped psych out some of the batters he subsequently faced, but it also backfired on him in retirement when he became eligible for the Baseball Hall of Fame.

"He'll never get my vote. He cheated and admitted it," one voter said.

Worried that his reputation as a spitballer might keep him out of Cooperstown, Perry tried to change the image of the illegal pitch—the spitball was outlawed in 1919—that he rode into the pitching fraternity's exclusive 300-win club. Asked if he would teach the spitball to the pitchers on the Limestone College baseball team he coached in Gaffney, South Carolina, Gaylord said, "They've got a new name for that pitch. It's called the split-fingered fastball, and it's legal."

Nobody was fooled by Perry's attempt to revise his mound history, but most voters didn't hold throwing the spitter against the big North Carolinian either. Perry was elected to the Hall in January of 1991, in his third year on the ballot.

DON
POLLARD

Ohio University history professor and author Charles Alexander tells a story that indicates that major leaguers, at least judging by Gaylord Perry, are pretty much like the rest of us.

Alexander is well known among baseball literature fans as the author of the definitive biography of Ty Cobb. In doing research for the book, Alexander visited Cobb's hometown of Royston, Georgia, several times. A few years later Royston decided to celebrate the centennial of Cobb's birth, and the sponsoring Royston Chamber of Commerce asked Alexander and Perry, who was coaching college baseball in nearby Limestone, South Carolina, to serve as co–grand marshals of a parade that was to be the highlight of the celebration.

On the morning of the parade Perry signed bats and balls at city hall, while Alexander signed copies of his Ty Cobb biography. Next, Perry, Alexander, and Alexander's wife, Jo Ann, were feted at a luncheon given by a small church college about three miles outside of Royston. After lunch they climbed into a stretch limousine that a car dealer in Atlanta had lent Royston for the occasion and headed back to town for the parade, being chauffeured by the president of Royston's only bank.

The three of them, dressed to the nines, were joking around and enjoying the slow ride back to Royston on the crowded two-lane highway when all of a sudden Perry shouted, "Look! There's a yard sale! Turn in there."

Alexander tried to remind Perry and his wife, who was also excited at the prospect of finding yard-sale treasures, about their impending engagement, but neither wanted to hear his words of caution. The bank president put on his left-hand turn signal but couldn't get an opening in the traffic coming from the opposite direction. As luck would have it, one of Royston's two police cars happened to be passing by. Recognizing the limousine and the bank president, the cop pulled off the road, stopped traffic on both sides of the highway, and waved the limousine into the driveway of the people having the yard sale.

Perry and Alexander's wife disappeared into the house, leaving Charles to make small talk with the startled man and woman who owned the property. "I'm Charles Alexander, and I teach at Ohio University," he said. "I'm down here for the Ty Cobb Centennial Celebration. The big fellow is Gaylord Perry. He's a famous baseball pitcher; retired a few years ago." The local couple had never heard of Perry, but they figured that their swanky guests, who were getting the royal treatment, must be important, so when Perry and Mrs. Alexander came out of the house the owners of the property had their three visitors pose on their front porch while they took a photo of them.

When Perry and the Alexanders were ready to resume their trip, the cop again stopped traffic for them in both directions so that the limousine could negotiate the turn back onto the highway. "We got into town in plenty of time to perform our duties in the parade," said Alexander, "but thank goodness neither Gaylord nor Jo Ann found something at the yard sale they just couldn't live without . . . like an antique dining room suite. I don't know what we'd have done with it if they had."

MIKE PIAZZA

Dodgers catcher Mike Piazza had a superb rookie season—he was a landslide winner of the National League Rookie of the Year Award in 1993—but he wasn't perfect.

On May 31 in St. Louis, Mike tried to nail a Cardinals baserunner stealing second, but his throw hit Dodgers pitcher Tom Candiotti in the rear end. Candiotti collapsed on the field because the ball actually hit him in a slightly lower, more vulnerable place than the buttocks. Once Candiotti recovered, he told manager Tommy Lasorda and trainer Charlie Strasser, who had rushed out to the mound to assist him, "You're not going to believe where it hit me."

This mishap rarely happens in professional baseball, and perhaps Candiotti could have done a better job of removing himself from Piazza's line of fire. Nevertheless, Piazza accepted full responsibility: "I guess it's funny now, but I could have hit him in the hand or the wrist or even the head. My intentions were good, but it was a stupid play."

The next day the rest of the Dodgers pitching staff gave Piazza a reminder to be more careful with his throws. The pitchers attached paper bull's-eyes to the seats of their baseball pants, surrounded Piazza, and then mooned him in concert.

THE PRESS BOX

Chicago sportswriter Jerome Holtzman once compiled a series of interviews he'd done with great American sportswriters into an oral-history book he titled *No Cheering in the Pressbox*. Holtzman's title refers to the unwritten rule that is designed to keep amateur hacks, guests, and freeloaders from acting like fans and thus disturbing the peace and quiet that is required by professional baseball journalists laboring under tight deadlines.

In the first World Series I covered I learned that this rule is taken very seriously indeed.

The 1984 Series pitted the Detroit Tigers against the San Diego Padres. The teams split the first two games in San Diego, but the Tigers swept the next three at home, displaying the combination of outstanding pitching, defense, and power hitting that had enabled them to dominate the American League with a 104–58 record. The play of the Tigers was so exciting that a few of the writers sitting near me in the Tiger Stadium auxiliary press box apparently forgot where they were and reacted like typical fans when Detroit's Marty Castillo hit a big two-run home run in the second inning of the third game.

Immediately, a reminder came over the PA system from Tigers publicity director Dan Ewald: "No cheering in the press box."

A short time later, as the third Tiger run of the inning crossed the plate, the same writers burst out again. This time

Ewald's words came as a rebuke: "No cheering in the press box!"

When the Tigers scored yet a fourth run in the inning and the incorrigible scribes cheered yet again, Ewald said not a word. With a policeman at his side, he confiscated the media credentials of the offending parties and escorted them from the press box. Needless to say, the proper working conditions prevailed throughout the press box for the duration of the Series.

Veteran Cincinnati Reds beat reporter Hal McCoy of the *Dayton Daily News* tells a story about the time he too was almost barred from the press box, not for cheering there, but for doing his job.

"Pitcher Tim Belcher was complaining one day about always having to watch out for the dog crap left behind on the field by owner Marge Schott's dog, Schottzie. I wrote about it in the paper, and Marge got so mad she barred me from the press-box dining room at Riverfront Stadium, where we writers traditionally received complimentary meals. She tried to bar me from the press box altogether, but the National League president, Bill White, said, 'No, you can't do that, Marge.'

"But she was able to keep me out of the dining room. When Belcher heard about it, he had some pizza delivered to me in the press box. Marge started barring other writers who wrote things she didn't like, so that pretty soon there were seven of us, 'the unwelcome seven,' who were not allowed into the dining room.

"We bought some white ball caps and had 'BARRED BY MARGE' and the slashed circle symbol meaning 'forbidden' imprinted on them. The hats became status symbols, and we had so many requests for them that we printed up extras and sold them to our colleagues.

"The caps were worn by almost everybody in the press box until Marge opened the dining room again to everyone, regardless of race, color, creed, or their penchant for writing stories critical of her and her policies . . . not because she had any change of heart, but rather because she decided she could make more money if she let everyone back in and started charging for the meals, which, as I said before, had traditionally been on the house, and which still are free in a lot of the ballparks around the league."

KIRBY PUCKETT

On July 12, 1996, Kirby Puckett announced that he was
retiring from baseball because of an irreparable vision
problem he was experiencing as a result of a beaning he suffered at the end of the 1995 season. Some observers immediately wondered if the premature ending of Puckett's 12-year
career would ruin his chances of being elected to the Baseball Hall of Fame. The doubts centered on Puckett's statisti-
cal totals, which, while very good, did not reach
"magic-number" accumulative levels that guarantee election.

Puckett supporters were unimpressed with such logic, to
say the least. They focused on Kirby's 10 straight All-Star
Game appearances, his six Gold Glove Awards, his .318 lifetime batting average, and the two World Championships he
led the Minnesota Twins to; and they pointed out that for a
solid decade Puckett was as good an all-around ballplayer as
could be found on the planet. Above all, there was the man
himself to consider. In an era of selfish, aloof players, Puckett, with his constant smile, friendliness, and infectious enthu-
siasm, stood out like a rose among weeds.

A number of people expressed the opinion that Puckett
would indeed make the Hall of Fame as soon as the standard
five-year waiting period was up, but Puckett's manager on the
Twins, Tom Kelly, said it best: "Why have a Hall of Fame if
you're not going to have Kirby Puckett in it?"

Contemporary athletes often have different ideas about their role in society from that of their predecessors. NBA star Charles Barkley, for example, stated point-blank that he was not a role model for kids and that, furthermore, he didn't want to be a role model. However, like it or not, professional athletes do have a tremendous influence on our young people. The lovable, irrepressible Puckett certainly did, as the following tale told by Patrick Ruesse of the *Minneapolis Star Tribune* illustrates. The story involves Puckett's former teammate, Randy Bush, an outfielder and designated hitter who played for the Twins from 1982 to 1993. It seems that Bush and his wife, Kathy, were having a very difficult time potty-training their two-year-old son, Ryan. The Bushes tried all the tricks, but nothing worked, not even the endorsement that "this is the way Daddy does it."

At wit's end, the Bushes finally thought to say, "This is the way Kirby does it."

The youngster's eyes widened with wonder: "Kirby does it?"

What's good enough for Kirby was good enough for Ryan, who was potty trained in no time.

DICK RADATZ

It's no wonder Dick Radatz was called "the Monster." At 6'5", 250 pounds, the fireballing reliever was an intimidating force on the pitcher's mound. Radatz also had a sense of humor.

At the end of his career Radatz found himself pitching for the expansion Montreal Expos. In a July 1969 game between the Expos and the Pirates, the Bucs' Dock Ellis hit the Expos' Mack Jones with a pitch, thereby touching off a typical baseball brawl: the kind of "fight" highlighted by lots of fulminating, posturing, and dancing around. Not to be left out of the theatrics, the huge Radatz bolted out of the Expos' dugout and raced up to Freddie Patek, the Pirates' 5'4", 145-pound shortstop, to deliver this classic line: "I'll take on you and a player to be named later."

REPLACEMENT PLAYERS

Spring training in 1995 began with the members of the Major League Players Association still on strike. The regular players' places in the spring games were taken by "replacement players": minor leaguers, free agents, and amateurs, who days before had been employed in routine occupations as truck drivers, salesmen, teachers, etc. Despite mockery from the media and threats of ostracism and retaliation from the striking major leaguers, the replacement players were motivated by the chance to realize the dream of playing baseball in the major leagues and by the promise of making some pretty good money: $5,000 for signing a contract, another $5,000 for being on the Opening Day roster, and $20,000 in severance pay if they were released after the start of the regular season.

On the eve of Opening Day, a federal judge ruled that the owners had violated the law in unilaterally abolishing free agency and salary arbitration and decreed that the prestrike rules governing baseball's labor-management relationship be reinstated. The regular players then called off their strike; the owners, unwilling to further alienate the public, declined to implement a lockout and postponed the start of the 1995 season by about three weeks.

Most of the owners also immediately canceled the contracts of their replacement players in order to avoid having to pay them $25,000 each in bonuses. Besides being yet another public relations gaffe, the move disgusted the replacement players, who felt cheated out of the money. Pitcher Tim Dell of the Milwaukee Brewers said, "It felt like it was our money already. The closer it got to Opening Day, the more we thought it was our money and the more it felt like if we didn't get it, they would be taking it from us."

In an unintentionally symbolic gesture, the Cincinnati Reds, who paid no bonuses, gave their departing replacement players plastic garbage bags in which to pack their personal gear.

Despite the general cheapness, a few owners showed they had hearts. Houston Astros owner Drayton McLane feted his 32 replacement players at a barbecue banquet around home plate at the Astrodome and gave each player a $10,000 check for dessert. "You have to treat people with respect and dignity. They uprooted their lives and gave it their best," said McLane.

Miami Marlins owner H. Wayne Huizenga was even more generous. He gave each of his replacement players the full $25,000 bonus, a kindness that cost him a total of $775,000.

DON
POLLARD

BRANCH RICKEY

Brooklyn Dodgers owner Branch Rickey was a religious and very moral man, but he had a reputation for being tight with a dollar. A master psychologist, Rickey also had no qualms about taking advantage of the other ball club when trading players, and few people ever got the best of him in negotiations of any kind.

One who did was Chuck Connors, who played briefly as a first baseman for Rickey, as well as for the Chicago Cubs, before becoming a famous cowboy actor on TV. One spring Connors was preparing himself to enter Rickey's office to talk contract when he ran into outfielder Gene Hermanski, coming out of Rickey's office. Hermanski told Connors: "Mr. Rickey asked me if I drank and when I told him 'just socially,' he wouldn't give me a raise."

Connors left Rickey's office with his raise secured because when Rickey popped his moralistic question, Connors said indignantly, "Mr. Rickey, if I have to drink to be on this team, I don't want any part of it."

Bobby Bragan, a backup catcher for the Brooklyn Dodgers for parts of four seasons, also remembers Rickey as a shrewd negotiator . . . and as a whole lot more.

"Mr. Rickey had the most amazing vocabulary of any man I've ever known," says Bragan, "and he was a spellbinding conversationalist. He could talk brilliantly on any number of subjects. He was a genius. Next to God, Mr. Rickey was Number One. That's how impressive an intellect he had. I tried to outfox Mr. Rickey one time about money, but only once.

"After the 1942 season I was traded from the Philadelphia Phillies to the Dodgers, and I was ecstatic about it. I was going from a last-place team and penny-pinching outfit to a first-class operation with a team that would contend for the pennant. I felt certain that my new team would want to give me a nice raise, but Mr. Rickey said that no, the Dodgers would pay me the same thing Philadelphia had because I was going to sit on the bench in Brooklyn and back up all the star players the Dodgers had.

"Well, when the 1943 season started, I was the first-string catcher and caught something like 50 of the first 52 games. In my mind this was grounds for renegotiating, since Mr. Rickey's refusal to give me a raise had been based on his prediction that I'd be a benchwarmer. I went up to Mr. Rickey's office at Ebbets Field, but his secretary said that he wasn't in and that I should come back tomorrow. The next day I did return, and as soon as I entered his office Mr. Rickey said, 'Bobby, my secretary told me that you came to see me yesterday. I stayed up most of the night worrying and trying to figure out what it is you want to see me about. And I prayed to God that you were not coming here to request more money, because either you're the kind of man who can live up to a contract or you're not. Isn't that right, Bobby?'

"'You're exactly right, Mr. Rickey,' I said. 'I just came by to say hello, that's all.'"

Bragan tells another story that beautifully illustrates Rickey's keen insight into human nature.

"Every spring Mr. Rickey would gather together all the men who were slated to manage teams in the Dodgers' farm system and tell them this story:

"A man stepped off a train and walked up to an old man sitting in a chair outside the station.

"'What kind of town is this?' asked the stranger.

"'It's a screw-you, me-first, down-and-dirty, every-man-for-himself kind of town,' answered the old man. The stranger nodded, left the train station, and found out that that's exactly the kind of town it was.

"The next day another stranger stepped off the train, and he too walked up to the same old man and asked him, 'What kind of town is this?'

"The old man said, 'It's a caring, generous, unselfish, brotherly-love kind of town.' The second man also found the town to be exactly as described.

"And just like the two strangers in this story, you, Mr. Manager, are going to make the town you go to."

JOSE RIJO

Baseball can be a cruel business. As long as you produce, you are held close to the bosom of the ball club; stop producing, though, and it's a different story entirely, as Jose Rijo of the Cincinnati Reds discovered in a rather bizarre and humiliating way.

From 1990 through half of the 1995 season, Rijo was the unquestioned ace among the Reds' starting pitchers. Unfortunately, in 1995 Jose suffered a recurrence of an old elbow injury, and on August 22, he had an operation on the arm that shelved him for the remainder of the season. Unable to pitch, Rijo spent the rest of the season in the Reds' dugout, cheering on his teammates and serving as a concerned big brother and informal coach to Hector Carrasco, the talented but immature and very young relief pitcher who, like Rijo, hails from the Dominican Republic.

Even without Rijo the Reds managed to win the mediocre National League Central Division and the right to play the Western Division–winning Los Angeles Dodgers in the newly expanded league playoffs. Despite his inability to pitch, Rijo still felt like a part of the team . . . that is, until the Reds failed to invite him to accompany the team to Los Angeles, where the playoffs opened on October 3. It seems there wasn't enough room for Rijo on the Reds' chartered plane. Inactive players Brian Hunter, Tim Pugh, and Damon Berryhill made the trip, though, as did two special nonplaying guests of owner Marge Schott: a life-size stuffed St. Bernard and a life-size stuffed elephant who together took up four seats on the chartered aircraft.

While the Reds were in L.A. preparing for Game 2 of the series against the Dodgers, Rijo sat at home in Cincinnati and unloaded his feelings to the press. "Can you believe it?" he asked. "They didn't even invite me. I didn't even get a call. I'm very pissed off. I should be there, not only for Hector but for everyone else. I felt I could've contributed by working with the guys, but now I won't be able to share what they're going through. After all I've been through with the organization, it's still a one-way street. My services are there for them, but they're not there for me. I feel like they don't consider me part of the team anymore."

Forced to address the issue of why the Reds' best pitcher for five-plus seasons was left behind, Reds general manager Jim Bowden offered a lame excuse: "Jose has not asked me about it. Had he, I'm sure we could have worked something out."

Rijo did not buy this explanation one bit and clearly blamed the Reds' insulting neglect of him on the club's storied cheapness regarding all things, excepting perhaps the salaries of key players: "They have $15 million invested in me and they're worried about $70 for a hotel room? I'd pay for half the room if they wanted me to and forget the meal money. I don't need that. So, what are they saving, $70?"

Rijo was so upset at being bumped off the Reds' charter by two stuffed animals that he refused the team's offer to appear on the field in uniform for introductions prior to the Reds' first home game of the playoffs. He bought a ticket and sat up in the grandstands with the rest of the paying customers.

MICKEY RIVERS

Fleet-footed, bowlegged Mickey Rivers, who played center field for the Angels, Yankees, and Rangers (1970–84), was an excellent leadoff hitter and a fine base stealer. He was also a flake of the first order who constantly kept his teammates in stitches by saying and doing off-the-wall things.

Rivers called people "gozzlehead" and "warplehead" (he said he heard the names in the ghetto) and once said a certain coach was so ugly that "your clothes wrinkle when he walks by."

Rivers expressed his fatalistic view of life this way: "Ain't no sense worrying about things you got no control over, 'cause if you got no control over them, ain't no sense in worrying. And ain't no sense worrying about things you got control over, 'cause if you got control over them, ain't no sense worrying."

Teams put Rivers in charge of their kangaroo courts just to see what Mickey would say and do. All-Star third baseman Buddy Bell remembers the time he was hauled up before Rivers, presiding over the Texas Rangers' kangaroo court.

Rivers said, "Mr. Bell, you are accused of throwing your batting helmet three times. How do you plead?"

"Guilty," said Bell.

"OK. That's three helmets at $2 a helmet," said judge Rivers. "Three and two is five, so you owe the court $5."

Years later, when Bell was winding down his career as a member of the Cincinnati Reds, he says he received a long-distance phone call from Miami, Florida. "This is Milton Waters," said the caller.

"Who?" asked Bell.

"Milton Waters," said the caller again.

"I'm sorry, I don't know any 'Milton Waters,'" said Bell, in a voice that indicated he was about to hang up.

"Buddy, don't hang up! It's me, Mickey," said Rivers. "I'm calling incognito."

Buddy explains it this way: "Mickey's middle name is 'Milton,' he's from Miami, and he just figured I'd get the connection between 'Rivers' and 'Waters.' Why was he calling 'incognito' in the first place? Who knows. That's just Mickey."

PHIL RIZZUTO

Over the years I've listened to some memorable National Baseball Hall of Fame induction speeches from the likes of Richie Ashburn, Johnny Bench, Steve Carlton, Ray Dandridge, Rollie Fingers, Catfish Hunter, Reggie Jackson, Tom Seaver, Mike Schmidt, Willie Stargell, Billy Williams, and Carl Yastrzemski.

The hands-down best speech I've ever heard at Cooperstown, because it was the funniest, was Phil Rizzuto's. It took little Phil, the former New York Yankees shortstop nicknamed "the Scooter," a long time to make the Hall, primarily because his batting record, though good, was not great. Rizzuto himself always thought that if and when he went into the Hall of Fame, he would go in with former Brooklyn Dodgers shortstop Pee Wee Reese, his rival throughout the 1950s and the player Rizzuto has always been closely compared to. When Reese was selected for induction in 1984, and Rizzuto wasn't, Rizzuto figured his own selection was never going to happen.

Ten years later it did happen, and so on July 31, 1994, there was Rizzuto, the longtime radio voice of the Yankees, standing on the dais in front of a sea of baseball fans with 33 baseball immortals, now his colleagues, seated behind him, and giving his Hall of Fame acceptance speech.

Although I'd never heard Rizzuto do a Yankees radio broadcast, I knew he had a reputation for zany non sequiturs, comic malapropisms, and maddening digressions. All of these surfaced and commingled in his remarks, which resembled a standup comedy routine as much as they did a speech. From the very start Rizzuto had everyone laughing, as he dropped one-liner after one-liner and even self-critiqued his rambling speech as he went along: "This is going nowhere! You see how I do this! I get sidetracked, then I don't know where I was going. See, I did it again! Oh, listen, anytime you want to leave, go ahead."

When Rizzuto said this, Johnny Bench and Yogi Berra stood up and walked off the stage, as if they were taking Rizzuto at his word. But of course they came back, because they wanted to hear the rest of Rizzuto's remarks too.

The funniest part of the speech may have been Rizzuto's recollections about his first year in professional baseball with a Yankees farm team in the small town of Bassett, Virginia. In speaking about what was his first trip into the South, Rizzuto recalled ordering supper on the train and finding some strange white stuff on his plate. But then he couldn't remember the name of the food and turned around to ask for help from Bill White, the National League president and Rizzuto's former broadcast partner with the Yankees.

"Grits! Yeah, grits," said Rizzuto. "That's the stuff. Anyway, so I see this stuff on my plate, and hey, I'm a kid from Brooklyn! I don't know about this stuff. So I put a handful in my pocket.

"So we get to Bassett, and I get out, and I don't see anything but farmland. Then the train pulls away, and there, behind the train, was the town. The population was 1,600 . . . including the cows.

"Playing for Bassett I hurt my leg, and gangrene set in. The doctors had to operate on it, but I was OK. And I think the gangrene really helped me get to the majors, because before that I was too fast and kept running by balls at short. The injury slowed me up just enough."

BROOKS ROBINSON

Modern-art critics do not think much of the work of Norman Rockwell. The critics don't like Rockwell because he was primarily a commercial illustrator whose work was most often used as magazine covers or advertisements; because he painted in a representational style (i.e., he painted scenes of people, places, and things that look like the real world); and because his paintings reflect the Judeo-Christian values of the American middle class. Average Americans, on the other hand, have always loved the artist and his work and continue to regard it as a classic American treasure.

Rockwell used baseball as the subject matter of several major paintings, and one of those paintings was sold at a Sotheby's auction on December 1, 1994, the centennial year of Rockwell's birth. The painting, titled *Gee, Thanks Brooks*, shows a young Brooks Robinson gladly signing a baseball for a young, wide-eyed Baltimore Orioles fan sitting in the first row of the grandstands. Commissioned in 1971 and used as an advertisement by Rawlings Sporting Goods, *Gee, Thanks Brooks* is one of the last large color canvases completed by Rockwell before his death. Brooks Robinson was the perfect subject for this painting, for it was his personal qualities—his humility and his graciousness—as much as his outstanding performance at the hot corner that endeared him to baseball fans everywhere.

The Sotheby auction house naturally undervalued the painting, estimating in its catalog that it would bring between $125,000 and $175,000. The final selling price was

$225,000, and the winning bidders turned out to be Brooks Robinson himself and his wife, Connie. The Robinsons bid anonymously, a precaution that may have caused them to pay more for the painting than necessary, as their main competitor said afterward that he would have backed off sooner had he known he was bidding against Brooks Robinson. In any case, while the Robinsons are not professional art critics, they certainly demonstrated that they recognize class when they see it.

ROOKIES

Being able to get friends and family into the ballpark free is just one of the many fringe benefits that go along with being a major league ballplayer. Each player typically gets four free passes to every game. Sometimes, though, those complimentary passes can be a real headache. That's because at certain times, particularly the postseason, players get far more requests for freebies than they can supply; moreover, the requests often come from distant relatives and acquaintances who haven't been heard from since the player was in diapers.

Rookies making their first appearances in their hometowns can also be besieged with requests for passes. In this case, however, it's much easier to acquire a supply of tickets from teammates who have no need for their allotted passes. When San Francisco pitcher John Burkett, who grew up in Beaver, Pennsylvania, made his first trip as a Giant to Three Rivers Stadium in Pittsburgh on May 25, 1990, he left 137 passes for family and friends at the Will Call ticket window. Needless to say, Burkett's largesse set a new club record.

In general, today's major league ballplayers may be more sophisticated and better educated than the ballplayers of generations ago, but rookies always seem to act like rubes.

Take the case of young Cincinnati Reds pitcher Steve Foster, who was called up to the big leagues for the first time during the first week of September 1991. Making his first trip out of the country, Foster flew into Montreal to join his teammates, who were playing a three-game series against the Expos.

When a Canadian customs agent at the airport asked Foster if he had anything to declare, the rookie said in all sincerity, "I declare that I'm proud to be an American."

On the Los Angeles Dodgers' first trip into Chicago during the 1994 season, Dodger veterans pulled a prank on one of their rookies that is a favorite of clubs around the National League. The veterans told 20-year-old Mexican pitcher Ismael Valdez about an initiation rite he would have to undergo to purge himself of his rookie status. His task: paint the private parts on a statue of a horse in the park across the street from the club's Chicago hotel.

Under the cover of darkness, Valdez stole into the park, spray-painted the "anatomically correct" parts of the horse Dodger blue, and then returned to the hotel, where his teammates congratulated him for graduating into their ranks.

The next day three uniformed Chicago policemen entered the Dodgers' clubhouse at Wrigley Field. They marched slowly and purposefully right toward Valdez's locker. Once there, they arrested the rookie pitcher on charges of vandalizing public property. The cops read Valdez his rights, handcuffed him, and proceeded to take him to jail. As Valdez was being led away, he looked around the clubhouse for support, but no one took the slightest notice of his predicament.

After walking the distressed pitcher halfway down a flight of stairs, the cops, who had been in on the prank from the beginning, had Valdez pause on the landing so he could hear the raucous laughter coming from the Dodgers' clubhouse.

PETE ROSE

A Cincinnati Reds team flight once flew right into the middle of a terrible thunderstorm. The plane encountered horrific turbulence, scaring even the veteran flight attendants and members of the crew. As his teammates prayed and struggled not to succumb to motion sickness, Pete Rose looked at seatmate Hal King and said with a big grin, "If this plane goes down, I'm taking a lifetime .300 batting average with me. How about you?"

Pete Rose had better-than-average physical abilities, but he was not a gifted athlete. What set him apart and enabled him to achieve one of the greatest records in all of sports (a career hit total of 4,256) was his intense, unrelenting drive and complete dedication to the game of baseball. Rose was the quintessential professional ballplayer, and his sense of professionalism extended even to how he wore his uniform . . . both on and off the field, as an unsuspecting publicity department employee of a major New York City book publisher found out the hard way.

Rose was doing a shoot in a downtown Cincinnati photography studio to obtain a photo for the dust jacket of the biography on which he and Roger Kahn were collaborating.

Rose was very cooperative, and the photographer was having a good time joking around with him. After the photographer took a couple of dozen pictures of Rose in various poses, the New York publicist swiveled Rose's Reds cap around so that the bill was pointing backward and said, "Let's try a couple of shots like that to show your lighter side."

Rose instantly turned sober, jerked the bill of his cap back to the front, and snapped, "No way! I never, ever wear a baseball uniform like a clown."

When former bonus baby Bob Bailey was winding down his 17-year major league career, he became a part-time player for the Cincinnati Reds in 1976 and 1977. By that time Bailey had begun to widen around the waistline, and his teammates on the Reds noticed that he was usually one of the first players to attack the postgame spread in the clubhouse.

One day Bailey was playing left field, and the batter hit a long fly over his head. Bailey went back to the fence, reached up, and barely missed catching the ball, which fell over the fence for a home run. After the game, sportswriter Bob Hertzel asked Rose if Bailey should have been able to catch the ball.

Rose looked Hertzel squarely in the eye and said, "If it had been a sandwich he would have caught it."

Cincinnati has had a long and glorious baseball history, but the city was never more proud of one of its players than it was of Pete Rose on September 11, 1985, when Rose broke Ty Cobb's record for most career hits. Jumping on the Pete Rose bandwagon, the Cincinnati city council quickly voted to rename Second Street, the thoroughfare that runs alongside Riverfront Stadium, "Pete Rose Way." "It's a great way to celebrate what makes us Cincinnati: hard work, determination, and aggressiveness," said City Councilman J. Kenneth Blackwell.

Everybody may have been proud of Pete Rose, but not everybody thought that the city council's idea was a good one. Some people saw a risk in naming a street after a living person who could wind up embarrassing the city. Of course, that's exactly what happened later when Rose was accused of betting on baseball; when he was banned from the game by Commissioner Bart Giamatti (even though the allegations against him were never proved); when he was convicted (in a separate matter) of income tax evasion; and when he served five months in a federal prison.

After Rose took his punishment like a man, most fans were inclined to forgive and forget. Others, convinced that Rose had indeed bet on baseball games (including games involving the Reds when he managed the team), remained unforgiving. Among those in the latter camp was Johnny Bench, the great catcher who had always resented having to share the spotlight with Rose during the glory days of Cincinnati's Big Red Machine. When fans at the 1995 Hall of Fame inductions chanted, "We want Pete! We want Pete!" Bench was heard to say, "You can have him." A few months later the host of a Cincinnati talk radio show succeeded in getting Bench and Rose to take turns sniping at each other over the airwaves. Bench said that Rose should confess he bet on baseball. Rose said that he couldn't understand why a supposedly intelligent guy like Bench kept on saying such stupid things. The Rose-Bench feud was reminiscent of the one that caused Babe Ruth and Lou Gehrig not to speak to each other for five years (the Ruth-Gehrig feud was actually the result of a minor spat between Ruth's wife, Claire, and Gehrig's mother).

At this point, in an attempt to symbolically bridge the gap between the two baseball superstars, Cincinnati city councilman Nick Vehr suggested that Pete Rose Way be renamed "Pete Rose/Johnny Bench Way." Vehr's idea was shot down, in large part because of a *Cincinnati Enquirer* editorial that reminded everybody that the objections against the original renaming of the street had proved to be prophetic. The *Enquirer* also pointed out that if the city got back into the business of renaming streets, it would be faced with demands to honor an unending stream of deserving players and teams.

Although Bench didn't get his city street, he did become the first Reds player to have his uniform number officially retired. In a long-overdue ceremony at Riverfront Stadium on September 1, 1996, Bench said, "This is just a stepping-stone to other numbers that need to be retired." Bench was right, but he probably did not have Rose in mind when he said this. As for Reds fans, they just wanted Bench and Rose to hug and make up, as Babe Ruth and Lou Gehrig finally did on "Lou Gehrig Appreciation Day" at Yankee Stadium, when Gehrig was dying from amyotrophic lateral sclerosis, or "Lou Gehrig's disease."

NOLAN RYAN

When batters suspect that they have been plunked intentionally by pitchers, they often try to hit back during unauthorized trips to the pitching mound. During his long career, Nolan Ryan used the inside part of the plate, and he hit his share of batters, but few people ever accused him of being a headhunter. Los Angeles Dodgers first baseman Pedro Guerrero certainly didn't. In fact, when a Ryan lightning bolt of a fastball cracked Guerrero's batting helmet in a 1983 game, Guerrero didn't even consider storming the mound to retaliate. Instead, Guerrero was so happy just to be alive that after the game he asked Ryan to autograph the helmet.

Only two players ever charged the mound after being hit by a Ryan fastball: Dave Winfield of the San Diego Padres and Robin Ventura of the Chicago White Sox.

Winfield went after Ryan, pitching for the Houston Astros at the time, during a game in 1980. Before he was pulled away, the big outfielder took a number of wild, ineffectual swings at Ryan, who fell to the ground and curled up in the fetal position to protect his pitching arm. Though physically unhurt, Ryan was embarrassed at his reaction and vowed that he would respond differently to the same situation in the future.

The opportunity didn't come until 13 years later (by which time Ryan was a member of the Texas Rangers), when Ryan nicked Chicago third baseman Robin Ventura on the elbow with a pitch. As Ventura charged the mound, he lowered his head to tackle Ryan, but Nolan adroitly caught him in a head-

175

lock and proceeded to bang him repeatedly on the top of the head with his fist. A benches-clearing brawl ensued and separated Ryan and Ventura; when order was restored, the umpires threw Ventura, but not Nolan, out of the game. Afterward, a few people criticized Ryan, but most people felt he was entirely justified in defending himself and found humor in the image, repeatedly shown on TV sportscasts, of Ryan giving Ventura what appeared to be a Three Stooges–type noogies massage.

One of Ryan's most impressive accomplishments is his record seven no-hitters. By definition, a pitcher is always tough when he throws a no-hitter, but Ryan was at his most dominating on the night of July 15, 1973, when, as a California Angel, he fired the second of his string of gems, against the Detroit Tigers.

Ryan struck out 17 batters in the game and might have struck out several more except for an Angels five-run rally in the top of the eighth inning. The rally, during which the Tigers changed pitchers three times, kept Ryan on the bench for almost 30 minutes and caused his shoulder to stiffen up. Although Ryan fanned weak-hitting shortstop Eddie Brinkman to open the eighth, he had lost enough that the Detroit hitters avoided whiffing while making the last five outs.

First baseman Norm Cash was Detroit's last hope. Ever the wise guy, the grinning Cash acknowledged the futility of batting against the "Ryan Express" by walking up to the plate holding not a bat but a wooden table leg. Oddly enough, home-plate umpire Ron Luciano didn't even notice that Cash wasn't holding a Louisville Slugger until a laughing Ryan pointed it out to him. Using a regulation bat, Cash managed only a blooper, which Angels shortstop Rudy Meoli caught easily to end the game.

After the game, a group of kids came up to Tigers players leaving the ballpark and asked for broken bats. Catcher Duke Sims, whom Ryan had fanned three out of three times, said, "Did you watch the game? We didn't hit the ball hard enough to crack any bats."

Nolan Ryan has so many fans not just because he was a great pitcher but also because he is a great person. According to Texas Rangers marketing director Dave Fendrick, "Nolan is the nicest, most humble superstar you'd ever want to meet. He also has a sense of humor.

"For example, one spring training when Bobby Valentine was managing the Rangers, Nolan was eating lunch in a restaurant in Port Charlotte, Florida. As Nolan was leaving the restaurant with his family, he noticed Valentine just sitting down. Nolan went over to his table to say hello, and when he left he said, 'Bobby, be sure to try the peach cobbler. It's the best I've ever had.'

"When Valentine finished his meal, the waitress asked him if he wanted any dessert. Valentine said, 'Yeah. I'll have the peach cobbler. I've heard it's pretty good.'

"The waitress said, 'It is delicious, but I'm sorry, sir, Nolan Ryan was here about an hour ago and he ate the last peach cobbler for the day.'"

To get some idea of how popular Nolan Ryan really is, especially in his home state of Texas, consider what happened when the Rangers announced that anyone named in his honor would be allowed to parade around the field before a game as part of Nolan Ryan Appreciation Week festivities held in 1993 at Arlington Stadium. All fans under the age of 27 (the number of years that Ryan played in the big leagues) who had been named either "Nolan" or "Ryan" were eligible to participate in the promotion. The Rangers figured on a couple of hundred participants, but close to 1,000 Nolans and Ryans (including a set of twins named Nolan and Ryan) showed up, carrying homemade banners and signs and wearing Nolan Ryan T-shirts and jerseys.

"We started out checking IDs and birth certificates to make sure that the participants had really been named after Nolan," says Fendrick, "but the response was so overwhelming we gave up on that. After a few minutes it was all we could do just to line them up and keep them moving around the field on the warning track in a semi-orderly fashion. Nolan was sitting in the Rangers' dugout, and as the people walked by he smiled and waved at them. It was an unbelievable sight, all those people, mostly males but a few females too, from little kids to adults, all named after Nolan, parading around Arlington Stadium."

One of the most amazing things about Ryan is the length of time he remained a dominating pitcher. Not only did Nolan pitch a record seven no-hitters (Sandy Koufax is the closest to Ryan with four), but he also pitched the first and last no-hitters nearly 20 years apart. The final out in Ryan's seventh no-hitter on May 1, 1991, was made by Toronto second baseman Roberto Alomar, Ryan's 16th strikeout victim of the game. Roberto's father, Sandy, played second base for the Angels behind Nolan when he pitched his first no-hitter on May 15, 1973. Later, after Sandy was traded to the New York Yankees, he became Ryan's 1,500th strikeout victim. Altogether, Nolan struck out five more father-son combinations, as well as 11 brother combinations.

In Ryan's great 27-year career he set more major league records than any other player in baseball history. Nolan even set a record after he was no longer playing. When both the Texas Rangers and the Houston Astros retired his uniform number (#34) in September of 1996, Ryan became the first player ever to have the honor bestowed on him by three different major league teams, as the California Angels had already retired his number back in 1992.

SALARY NEGOTIATIONS
AND CONTRACTS

In the old days when they were paid salaries, and not chunks of the GNP, ballplayers routinely negotiated their own contracts. One year New York Yankees outfielder Lou Piniella was haggling with New York general manager Gabe Paul over a few thousand dollars. Over a dinner in a Chinese restaurant Paul suggested that they split the difference between the amount Piniella was seeking and the amount the Yankees were offering. After the meal, while Piniella was mulling over the offer, Paul had fortune cookies delivered to the table. Piniella cracked open his cookie to find a message that read, "Be happy with what you have."

Knowing when he was beaten, Piniella accepted Paul's offer.

When first baseman Will Clark played for the San Francisco Giants, there wasn't a whole lot he could do in the off-season to stay in shape. His contract forbade his participation in 53 specific sports and recreational activities, everything from auto racing and kayaking to tennis and wood chopping. You can't blame the Giants for trying to protect their investment in their "franchise" player, but the experience of Kansas City Royals pitcher Steve Crawford makes you think that maybe the Giants should have banned the spectating of sports too.

Crawford and teammate George Brett were attending a Kansas City Blades hockey game in the winter of 1991 when an errant slap shot flew into the crowd and struck Crawford in the right side of the head. Although Crawford was not knocked unconscious, he was taken for precautionary x-rays to the hospital, where he issued a statement worthy of Dizzy Dean. "It would have killed a normal person," said Crawford.

Young players have little leverage in salary negotiations. They can complain to the press and hint about holding out or quitting baseball, but they inevitably accept nominal raises and show up ready to play in the spring. This didn't stop relief pitcher Bobby Thigpen from using a unique bargaining stratagem after his excellent first full season in the majors (7–5, 16 saves).

In complaining about the contract he was being offered for 1988 (a jump from $62,500 to $70,000), Thigpen tried to seduce White Sox chairman Jerry Reinsdorf with poetry:

> As I sit home this off-season,
> I wonder what the hell is the reason,
> Why the club wants to be unfair,
> Underpaying a player who can produce and care.

Although the literature department at Mississippi State University, where Thigpen had starred as a collegiate player, must have been proud to see a former Bulldog put poetry to such practical use, the amused Reinsdorf simply fought back with some doggerel of his own:

> I hope you are really a good pitcher,
> Because as a poet you'll never get richer;
> If you're not pitching this year,
> I will be sad but won't fear;
> Though you may be one of the best,
> There's always someone among the rest.

In all, Thigpen (who wanted his salary doubled) sent Reinsdorf about a dozen "bargaining poems." They didn't win the pitcher any more money or any literary prizes, but they did show some improvement:

> It's true my potential as a poet is very small,
> But in the ninth who do you want to have the ball?
> You say there'll always be someone among the rest,
> But who do you want, them or the best?

I said *some* improvement.

When a player takes his salary demands to arbitration, both his representatives and those of the ballclub ply the often-overwhelmed arbitrator with mountains of statistics, comparisons, and opinions in an effort to prove that the player is or is not worthy of the money he is seeking. With large sums of money, not to mention pride and countless hours of research, at stake, the ball clubs are sometimes brutally frank about players' weaknesses and limitations, while the players' representatives sometimes resort to trickery that borders on mendaciousness.

For example, during Chicago White Sox outfielder Gary Redus's arbitration hearing in the winter of 1988, Redus's representatives impressed the arbitrator with the information that their client's on-base percentage the previous season had been higher than his batting average.

Jack Gould, representing the White Sox, immediately called a "time-out" to point out that this was hardly a highlight to be emblazoned on a player's Hall of Fame plaque, since it is virtually impossible for a player's on-base percentage *not* to be higher than his batting average. As any halfway knowledgeable baseball fan knows, all a player has to do is draw one walk or be hit by a pitch one time all season and his on-base percentage will exceed his batting average.

Although Gould prevented Redus's reps from scoring an unearned run with the arbitrator, Redus still prevailed as the arbitrator decided that Redus's asking price of $460,000 was more fair than the team's bid of $370,000.

TIM SALMON

California Angels outfielder Tim Salmon, one of the most popular young players in the game today, was doing his best one day to cooperate with the strange requests of a film crew putting together a comic bit for their television show. Salmon did a number of tricks, including rolling up the sleeve of his jersey to show off his biceps muscle, but then the interviewer asked, "Is there any player whose home-run swing you can imitate?"

Salmon thought for just a second, then said, "No, there's not. I can't even imitate my own home-run swing often enough."

STEVE SAX

Maybe it wasn't the dreaded sophomore jinx, but something weird hit Los Angeles Dodgers second baseman Steve Sax in his second year in the majors in 1983. For some inexplicable reason his arm suddenly went bananas on him, and the simple toss to first on a routine ground ball almost became an impossibility. Some of Sax's pegs were ridiculously wild, and as word of his problem spread around the league he was made the butt of much kidding. Opposing players in the first-base dugout would scurry out of the line of fire when Sax cocked his arm for a throw to first, and fans held up signs that said, "Sax, throw me a souvenir!"

During hours of extra practice Sax threw perfectly to first, even when blindfolded, but in games his wildness continued. For the season Steve accumulated a league-high 30 errors, 28 of them the throwing variety.

Dodgers manager Tommy Lasorda tried to cure Sax's strange malady by boosting his confidence. "How many men are walking the streets of this great nation who can hit .280 in the major leagues like you're doing? Not many, right?" asked Lasorda.

"Right," said Sax.

"How many men out there can steal 50 bases in a season like you're doing? Not many, right?"

"Right," said Sax again.

"Well, then, how many men can make a simple toss from second to first? Millions. In fact, there's 10 million women who can do it! Right?"

Sax had to agree once again, but Lasorda's lighthearted logic didn't help him with his problem.

What finally did help Sax was a prank Lasorda and Dodgers coach Mark Crese pulled on the second sacker. One night while Lasorda diverted Sax in the hotel lobby, Crese put a big, greasy pig's head under the sheets in Sax's bed, in place of one of the pillows. Sax was startled when he discovered the pig's head and worried when he found a note attached that said: "Saxy, you better start bearing down and throwing the ball right—or else. Signed, The Godfather."

As Sax recounted the incident to him, Lasorda fought to stifle his laughter but lost all control when Sax asked him in all seriousness, "Do you think the note might've been from a guy who lost money on a game because I threw a ball away?"

Loosened up by all the laughter, Sax went errorless in the Dodgers' last 38 games.

MARGE SCHOTT

Contemporary players are hardly the only ones in baseball embarrassingly ignorant of baseball history. A woman once approached Cincinnati Reds owner and CEO Marge Schott on an airplane and introduced herself as Edd Roush's granddaughter.

Schott replied, "That's nice, hon. What business is he in?" Roush was not only elected to the Hall of Fame, but was also the greatest player to ever wear a Cincinnati Reds uniform, as determined by a poll of Reds fans. Roush's granddaughter's reaction to Schott's ignorance? "She doesn't know a thing about baseball or she would have heard of me. She shouldn't be an owner."

Throughout her tenure at the helm of the Reds, Marge often found herself in trouble for saying something offensive about a racial, ethnic, or sexual minority, and in July of 1996 she was suspended from baseball for the second time. Nevertheless, during the suspension Marge continued to make her presence known in the Reds' front offices, and the National League stepped in to make it clear that her suspension meant a complete and total ban. She would be able to attend Reds games, but she would have to buy a ticket the same as any other fan.

During Marge's banishment the Reds were run by interim CEO John Allen, who immediately courted disenchanted Reds fans by running a number of fan-friendly promotions, including a couple of $3 ticket nights. Schott did not like Allen's discounted ticket promotions because she felt they made her look bad. She needn't have worried. Her reputation for stinginess was already cast in stone.

When Pete Rose heard about the National League's pronouncement that Marge would have to buy a ticket in order to attend a Reds game, he said, "She'll probably wait for a $3 ticket night."

TOM SELLECK

Actor Tom Selleck has been a rabid Detroit Tigers fan all his life; the Tigers cap he always wore in the role of private investigator Thomas Magnum was not an arbitrarily chosen prop. In 1991 while preparing for the role of an aging American slugger playing in Japan in the movie *Mr. Baseball*, Selleck actually got to bat for his beloved Tigers, albeit in a spring training contest.

The Tigers, hosting the Reds in Lakeland, Florida, were ahead 4–2 with two out in the bottom of the eighth when Selleck pinch-hit for Rob Deer. The left-handed-batting Selleck, who later admitted, "My knees were shaking a little bit," stepped in to face the Reds' Tim Layana, a right-handed reliever. Selleck looked at Layana's first pitch for a ball; fouled the next pitch behind the Reds' dugout on the third-base side; swung at and missed a low, outside pitch; hit a second foul into the left-field stands; then struck out on a knuckle curve.

As plotted, Layana served the actor two change-ups, but Selleck fouled off both of them. The Reds didn't expect Selleck to hit Layana's last pitch. "It dropped off the table," said Reds catcher Jeff Reed. "That's a tough pitch to hit, even if you've seen it before." Despite the strikeout, Reed was impressed with Selleck, the Hollywood Bambino: "He swung the bat pretty good for an actor, didn't he?"

As for Selleck, he was just relieved that his participation hadn't "cost the Tigers a close game." Though their celebrity strikeout artist wasn't at fault, the Tigers did lose the game 6–4 after giving up four runs in the top of the ninth.

THE '68 TIGERS

Former Detroit Tiger Jon Warden pitched only one year in the major leagues, while Hank Aguirre pitched ten years for the Tigers, yet it was Warden who was in the right place at the right time.

"When I went to spring training in 1968," says Warden, "I only had two years of pro ball under my belt. I wasn't really thinking about making the big club, and I would have been happy to start the season in Triple A. But I got a big break in the sense that the Tigers had lost the pennant the year before by one game because of their bullpen. Their relief pitching had been terrible, and they had a lot of older guys in the bullpen: Johnny Podres, Al Worthington, Johnny Klippstein, Fred Gladding, and Hank Aguirre, who had been with Detroit for years.

"As spring training went along the Tigers released these older guys one after the other. They kept giving me the ball, and I kept getting people out. Hank Aguirre was the last of these older guys they got rid of—they sold him to the Dodgers—and when they did I started thinking, 'Hey, I've got a real shot at making this club.'

"Well, not only did I make the major league team, but we also went on to win Detroit's first pennant since 1945, and then we beat the St. Louis Cardinals in the World Series in seven games. So, after that, whenever somebody would say to Aguirre, 'Hey, Hank, too bad you just missed the Tigers' big year,' he'd say, 'Yeah, that damn Warden has *my* World Series ring.'"

The 1968 Tigers were a close-knit team of veterans, and some of them, such as pitcher Mickey Lolich, were not disposed to be hospitable to a rookie, such as Warden.

"I made my major league debut against the Boston Red Sox in the second game of the season," says Warden. "I relieved Lolich in the eighth inning with the game tied. The first batter I faced was Rico Petrocelli. Now, Ray Oyler was our shortstop. Ray couldn't hit the ocean standing 10 feet from the shore, but he could really pick it with the glove.

"Petrocelli hits a ground ball to short, and I'm thinking, 'Alright!' . . . but the ball goes right between Oyler's legs. The next guy gets a hit, I get a couple of outs, then I walk a guy, and all of a sudden the bases are loaded, and I'm thinking, 'Oh, man, I'm outta here, back to the minors.' But the next batter hits a fly ball to Willie Horton in left, and I'm out of the inning.

"We don't get any runs in the eighth, so I'm back out for the ninth. I retire Jerry Adair and Mike Andrews, which brings up Carl Yastrzemski. Bill Freehan, our veteran catcher, comes trotting out to the mound to deliver some real words of wisdom to me, the rookie. 'Don't let this guy beat us with the home run,' he says. And I'm thinking, 'Oh, really, Bill? No kidding! I thought I'd lay one right in there for him.' I go to 3–2 on Yastrzemski and then strike him out swinging on a slider for my first major league strikeout.

"In the bottom of the ninth I'm the leadoff hitter. But Gates Brown pinch-hits for me and knocks a home run into the upper deck off John Wyatt, and I'm 1–0. I go into the locker room, and the reporters naturally want to talk to me: 'How's it feel to be a rookie and win your first game? Were you nervous out there? What did you think about facing Yastrzemski in that situation? Blah, blah, blah.' I answer all their questions, and then Lolich, whose locker was next to mine, says, 'Aw, you're not that good, Warden. Your bubble will burst.' I thought he was just kidding, because I didn't know him very well, but he was really irritated.

"Well, two days later Cleveland comes to town. I go into the game in the ninth with a runner on and one out. On my first pitch the guy on first tries to steal. Freehan throws him out. On my next pitch Lee May flies out, and I'm out of the inning. In the bottom of the ninth Willie Horton hits a three-run homer, we win, and I'm 2–0. The reporters are over at my locker again, and Lolich is pissing and moaning: 'Ah, geez, you damn rookie, you're not any good. Your bubble will burst.'

"Then we go to Chicago. It's the bottom of the ninth, we're up by one, bases loaded, one out, and they bring me, a left-hander, in to face a left-handed hitter, Wayne Causey. I walk him on four pitches to bring in the tying run, so the starting pitcher, Joe Sparma, is mad about that. Ken Boyer is up next. The bases are still loaded with one out: one more run and the game's over. I'm waiting for our manager, Mayo Smith, to bring in a right-hander to face Boyer so we get a righty versus a righty. But nobody comes out, so I say to myself, 'I guess I'm it.'

"I throw Boyer a hanging slider, and, man, he hits a vicious line drive, but it goes right to the third baseman, Don Wert, who catches it and steps on the bag for a double play. Out of the inning. In the top of the 10th Willie Horton hits a two-run homer; Dennis Ribant comes in and pitches the 10th, gets the save; and I get the win. I'm 3–0!

"So now Lolich is going absolutely nuts: 'Ya, ya, ya . . . You're terrible, Warden! I can't believe the crap you're throwing up there.'

"I said, 'Gee, Mickey, let's see. I've made three appearances, I've pitched three and a third innings, and I'm 3–0. Damn, at this rate, I'll win 40 or 50 games this season.'"

Warden didn't win 40 games that year—in fact, he won just four—but Denny McLain, the ace of the 1968 Tigers' pitching staff, did win an amazing 31 games that year. (Warden likes to say, "Me and Denny won 35 games in 1968.") He remembers Denny McLain as the most outrageous and most unpredictable character on a team full of characters.

"I thought McLain was a real fun guy," says Warden. "He sure as hell liked to have fun. You probably remember that McLain played the organ in nightclubs. Well, Denny was scheduled to pitch the first game of the World Series, but the night before the game, where was Denny? Down in the hotel lounge, playing the organ until two in the morning. And we were playing a day game the next day, too. Hell, I knew I wasn't going to get off the bench, but I left the lounge by midnight and went to bed. Not Denny. He closed the place.

"People would ask me, 'How come you get along with McLain so well?' And I'd say, 'Well, he's already alienated everybody else on the team. I'm just a rookie, so he's breaking me in.' McLain was generous, too. He'd always pick up the check whenever we went out, which I appreciated because I was only making about 10 grand for the year. Denny was making at least 60.

"Another thing about Denny is that he was the worst cardplayer in the history of baseball. We had a card-playing team, and we played a lot of poker on the road, usually in Gates Brown and Willie Horton's room. You know this was in the old days because we all had roommates. These prima donnas today have suites all to themselves. Anyway, we'd always let McLain in the game because he was such a bad cardplayer. Pat Dobson nicknamed him 'the Dolphin' because he was such a fish. We'd be playing five-card stud, and McLain would have an ace, king, two, three . . . all different suits, and he'd look at his cards and say, 'Oh, let's see now . . . yeah, I'll call that 10-dollar raise.' And I'd be thinking, 'What in the hell is he

gonna make out of that damn hand? He ain't got a prayer for anything. He's four-suited and has no pairs.' But that was Denny."

McLain was at his most unpredictable the day Yankees star Mickey Mantle played his last game in Detroit. "We clinched the pennant on Tuesday night against the Yankees," says Warden. "The next day we got rained out, and thank God we did, because the whole team stayed up all night drinking champagne to celebrate. We had some guys who normally didn't drink at all, and they were passed out in the clubhouse on Wednesday.

"Thursday was supposed to have been an off-day, but we played to make up the rainout on Wednesday, even though we'd already clinched the pennant. McLain had been scheduled to pitch on Wednesday, so he went ahead and pitched on Thursday. It was an afternoon game, and we had a nice crowd: we were playing the Yankees, we'd just won the pennant, and everybody knew it was Mantle's last appearance in Detroit.

"McLain's throwing a shutout going into the seventh or eighth inning, and we've got the game won when Mantle comes up for his last time in Tiger Stadium. McLain calls Freehan out to the mound and says to him, 'Tell Mantle it's coming right down the middle. I want to see him hit one outta here one last time.' Freehan goes back to the plate and gives Mantle the message.

"Well, the Yankees all know how goofy McLain is, so Mantle says, 'Yeah, right.' But the first pitch is right down the middle, just like McLain said it would be, and Mantle fouls it off. Mantle looks out at Denny, and Denny nods at him. The next pitch is right down the middle too, and Mantle hits a rocket into the upper deck in right that curves just foul.

"So Mantle takes his right hand and holds it out over the plate to indicate to McLain, 'Just a little higher.'

"Now, McLain could thread a needle with his fastball, so he puts it right where Mantle had asked for it, and BOOM: Mantle hits that sucker a ton—upper deck, home run. And as Mantle runs around the bases Denny takes off his glove and claps for him; our second baseman, Dick McAuliffe, takes off his glove and claps too. Hell, the whole team was clapping.

"Joe Pepitone is up next. He digs in, looks out at Denny, and motions just like Mantle did: 'Put her right here, Denny, old boy.' McLain threw a fastball right at his ear hole and knocked him on his ass.

"After the game some of the writers who were worried about the integrity of the game and all that crap were all over Denny: 'Did you let Mantle hit that home run?' So Denny had to deny it: 'Oh, no. I really juiced that ball. Mantle just had a helluva swing.' We all knew different."

GEORGE STEINBRENNER

Everyone who has ever been in the employ of New York Yankees owner George Steinbrenner has been subject to being fired in a "New York minute," especially managers. Steinbrenner's having changed managers 18 times in 17 years is surely one of baseball's most dubious records.

Steinbrenner's extraordinary impatience as boss even caused a moment of levity during the trial of Howard Spira, whom Steinbrenner accused of trying to extort money from him. At one point in the trial, Spira's lawyer asked Steinbrenner, merely for the record, if Lou Piniella had been manager of the Yankees in late 1988. Steinbrenner's reply of "He may have been" brought chuckles from nearly everyone in the courtroom.

DON
POLLARD

CASEY STENGEL

Longtime San Diego Padres radio announcer Jerry Coleman played for Casey when Stengel was managing the Yankees in the 1950s and says that a lot of the funny things Casey said and did came out of his understanding that "you have to promote your business."

"Stengel may have played the fool sometimes, but he was smart," says Coleman. "For instance, if a reporter came up to him and said, 'Who's better at second base, Jerry Coleman or Billy Martin?' . . . Casey wasn't going to answer that question. He was too smart for that. No matter what he said, one guy was going to be mad.

"So, what Casey would do is start talking about the first guy: 'Coleman can do this and he's good at that, and so on and so forth.' And then he'd talk about the second guy: 'Now, Martin is good at this and he can do that, and so on and so forth,' and he'd just keep going on and on so that pretty soon you're back to John McGraw and you've forgotten what your question was.

"Other times, when the situation called for it, Casey would get directly to the point and be clear as day.

"I remember Don Larsen's perfect game in the '56 World Series. In the top of the eighth inning the guys on our bench were really getting into the game. They started going up to the top step of the dugout and waving this guy a few steps to the right and another guy a few steps to the left. And, right away, Stengel barks: "Sit down! I'm the manager. I'll tell 'em where to play."

Famous for platooning and developing position versatility in his players, Stengel knew how to best utilize each of his players, even when they weren't playing. Clarence Marshall, a pitcher with a 7–7 lifetime mark in the major leagues, remembers a story that illustrates this point.

"It was 1945, and I was a member of Casey's Kansas City Blues team in the American Association," says Marshall. "One day the home-plate umpire was having a terrible game calling balls and strikes, so I started yelling at him. The ump looked over at our dugout and told me to shut up. Casey said, 'Keep it up.'

"Well, Casey was my manager, so I obeyed him and started yelling again. The ump warned me again, and Casey said to keep it up again. I did, and this time the umpire threw me out of the game. As I walked past him on the way to the locker room, Casey said, 'Better *you* than me. I wasn't going to pitch you today anyway.'"

After the Yankees lost the 1960 World Series, Casey was fired as manager, ostensibly because he was too old. Casey's comment was: "I'll never make the mistake of being 70 again." That should have been the end of Casey's baseball career, but the New York Mets, born in 1962, needed a manager, and the Mets' brass figured Stengel would be good for the gate, if nothing else. Everyone's modest expectations for the new team turned out to be wildly exaggerated as the Mets proved to be the worst team in baseball history, capable of snatching defeat from the jaws of victory in innumerable, mind-blowing ways. Yet, with the entertaining, venerable

Stengel running the show, the Mets were adopted by New York as the city's lovable losers. Casey's three-and-a-half-year reign over the Mets became one of the funniest and most unlikely chapters in baseball history.

Heading into their inaugural season of play in the National League, the Mets in 1962 were running a little behind. In spring training they'd never gotten around to working on a pickoff play, so Casey decided to cover it in the team's first clubhouse meeting. With all his pitchers and catchers assembled in the Mets' locker room, Stengel threw a towel on the floor for first base and told catcher Chris Cannizzaro to pretend he was a baserunner. Halfway across the room Casey pretended he was a pitcher working from the stretch.

In the spirit of the demonstration, Cannizzaro took his lead, edging away from the towel in a crouched position, and jockeyed back and forth, while Casey launched into one of his patented long-winded, convoluted lectures. Five minutes later Casey was still talking, and Cannizzaro began to relax. Stengel rambled on for another five minutes, and Cannizzaro relaxed some more. Another five minutes passed with Casey preaching as vociferously as when he'd started.

By this time Cannizzaro was standing upright with his legs crossed, and he was half asleep. Suddenly, Stengel whirled toward Cannizzaro, made a throwing motion, and shouted, "Bam! Gotcha!"

The Mets howled with laughter for several minutes, after which Casey calmly proceeded with the lecture.

When he was inducted into the Baseball Hall of Fame former Philadelphia Phillies centerfielder Richie Ashburn recalled playing his last season in the majors with Stengel's 1962 Mets. As the only Mets player to bat over .300 for the year, Ashburn was voted the team's MVP. "I was voted the Most Valuable Player on the worst team in baseball history. I wasn't sure what to make of that," said Ashburn.

Ashburn remembers Stengel fondly, and he enjoyed telling a story that illustrates the "Old Professor's" heart.

"We were playing the Cubs on the last day of the season," said Ashburn. "It was the top of the eighth, and we were trailing, but we got a nice little rally going. Solly Drake opened the inning with a single, and then I hit one too. So we've got two guys on, nobody out. Our catcher, Joe Pignatano, was up next, and he hit a looper over second that looked like a sure base hit. Naturally, Solly and I both took off; however, the Cubs' second baseman, Kenny Hubbs, made a great over-the-shoulder catch for the first out and then threw to Ernie Banks at first for the second out. Ernie then threw to the Cubs' shortstop, Andre Rodgers, who stepped on second to double off Solly for the third out. It was a triple play, which was a perfectly appropriate symbol of how our entire season had gone. But it was another tough loss for us.

"So everyone was down as we filed into the clubhouse. Casey saw this and called everyone together. 'Fellas,' he said, 'don't feel bad about this season, which has been simply amazin'. No one or two of you could have done all this by yourselves. This was a total team effort.'"

DICK STUART

Dick Stuart had some pop in his bat but was much more renowned for his atrocious fielding as a first baseman.

After belting 42 home runs for the Boston Red Sox during the 1963 season, Stuart was being honored at a Hot Stove League banquet. In acknowledging the presence of his wife, Stuart said, "Behind every successful man stands a woman."

A female Red Sox fan in the audience stood up and shouted, "And if she's standing behind you, she'd better be wearing a first baseman's mitt."

TIGER STADIUM

Along with Wrigley Field, Fenway Park, and Yankee Stadium, Tiger Stadium is one of the last of the classic major league ballparks left standing. Baseball legends (from both leagues) too numerous to mention have played on Tiger Stadium's hallowed ground, and the park remains, despite its age, an incomparable place in which to experience a ball game, primarily because the grandstands at Tiger Stadium were built so close to the field that you can actually hear the players' chatter.

Unfortunately, this architectural and historical treasure has its enemies. Team owner Mike Ilitch, Tigers officials, local and state politicians, and influential members of the Detroit media have formed a coalition to condemn Tiger Stadium as an obsolete, unredeemable white elephant and to convince the public of the need for a new baseball stadium with many "revenue-enhancing" features. As powerful as they are, this coalition has not been unopposed. In 1987 a group of loyal Tigers fans formed a group called The Tiger Stadium Fan Club to work for the preservation of the old ballpark, and their efforts have been nothing less than heroic. Led by founding member Frank Rashid, The Tiger Stadium Fan Club has built a grassroots organization of more than 11,000 members, published a newsletter, devised an economical plan (The Cochrane Plan) for the renovation of Tiger Stadium, and argued for the preservation of Tiger Stadium at countless public hearings. The Tiger Stadium Fan Club even came up with the inspired idea of giving the old ballpark a giant hug on its birthday.

"Early in 1988," says Rashid, "we decided we needed some sort of big demonstration to highlight the importance of the stadium. Somebody got the idea of making a human chain around the stadium. We decided to call it a 'hug' even though that sounds a little sappy, because the symbolism of protecting the stadium was right.

"The Tigers fought us all the way, but they basically had to permit us to do it because the sidewalks around Tiger Stadium are public property. And city council approved the idea because they didn't want to interfere with our free-speech rights. We decided to do the hug before the Tigers' game on April 20, 1988, because that was the 75th anniversary of the opening of the park. Unfortunately, the weather was terrible. It was a cold and rainy day. We had set up a stage in a parking lot across the street from the stadium, and we had musical acts and a high-school band, and we were giving speeches. But there weren't many people showing up. We were getting real worried, but a lot of people showed up at the last minute, and a lot of other people had assembled on the other side of the ballpark.

"The night before, we'd had a big debate about whether people should be turned inward or outward as they hugged the stadium. As it turned out, we had people facing both ways as they linked arms and held hands. It took about 1,200 people to encircle the ballpark. We had marshals with walkie-talkies positioned at various points around the stadium, and when the circle for the hug was complete, one of the marshals said to me over the walkie-talkie, 'We're tight, Frank; we're tight.' I guess the hug lasted about two to three minutes.

"The Tiger Stadium Fan Club went into debt over this Stadium Hug. We had made up a lot of Tiger Stadium souvenirs, but we didn't sell many of them because the bad weather kept the crowds down. In fact, the game was called after two innings. Nevertheless, the hug gave us the boost in credibility that we needed. Our opponents used it to try to trivialize what we were doing—they started calling us 'stadium huggers' and 'nostalgia freaks'—but even they admitted that the hug was a public relations work of genius."

TRIVIA

Has anybody ever raked in a greater return on his base-ball trivia knowledge than Robert Heuer? Betting the uniform numbers of six of his favorite players, the 59-year-old resident of Flushing won two and a quarter million dollars in the New York State lottery in 1987. The numbers Heuer played were 5 (Joe DiMaggio), 16 (Whitey Ford), 24 (Willie Mays), 27 (Juan Marichal), 37 (Casey Stengel), and 44 (Willie McCovey).

It was probably just a coincidence, but Alan Ashby had to wonder if the folks at the Texas Division of Motor Vehicles were trying to make fun of his defensive abilities when he was a catcher for the Houston Astros. They sent him tags for his white Pontiac Fiero that read "E-2."

On the other hand, although he was an excellent catcher defensively, the Mariners' Dave Valle was such a weak hitter during the 1991 season (when he batted .194) that a Seattle bar pegged the price of beer to his batting average.

Naming children is always a tricky business. Parents invariably have different preferences and often disagree about whether common or unusual names are better. One way out of the dilemma is to name a child after an esteemed relative or public figure the parents admire. That's why some baseball fans name their kids after favorite players. Some might call them obsessive, but such fans are no more obsessive than parents who give all their kids names that begin with the same letter, as did the parents of journeyman third baseman Vance Law. Vance's mom, VaNita, and his dad, Vernon Law, a former big-league pitcher with the Pittsburgh Pirates, apparently fell in love with the letter "V." They named Vance's brothers and sisters Veldon, Veryl, Vaughn, Varlin, and VyLynda.

THE UGLY
AMERICAN WORLD SERIES

The 1992 World Series was an especially historic event as the Atlanta Braves and Toronto Blue Jays squared off in the first international World Series in baseball history; however, when a U.S. Marine color guard marched into Atlanta–Fulton County Stadium carrying the Canadian flag upside down before Game 2, the American-Canadian harmony spurred by baseball's showcase event was momentarily disrupted.

Although the upside-down Maple Leaf was not shown on American TV, millions of Canadian viewers saw it and called Canadian radio and TV stations, newspapers, and government offices to protest. A Marine Corps spokesman called the blunder unintentional, and Major League Baseball quickly issued an apology, but Canadians were not immediately pacified, and the next day the Canadian press was highly critical of what it deemed to be typical American misbehavior. "The flag gaffe speaks to the appalling ignorance many Americans suffer whenever it comes to dealing with any country other than their own," said the *Toronto Sun*. "That's one of the reasons that, despite their best intentions, they so often end up being hated even by those they genuinely want to help." Ouch! At least the *Sun* injected some humor into its sarcasm when it asked: "What did the Marine color guard believe was on the Canadian flag when it was placed on the pole? The Canadian version of home plate? A Rorschach test for Deion Sanders? The costume Jane Fonda wore in *Barbarella?*"

With Games 3 through 5 scheduled for Toronto, the potential was there for the issue to become as blown out of proportion as the million-dollar salary of a .200-hitting benchwarmer. A call went out for Blue Jays fans to attend Game 3 carrying American flags upside down, but fortunately a majority of Jays fans opted instead to wave Canadian flags with a message attached to the top of each flag: "This end up." The Canadians also gave the U.S. Marine Corps another chance. While a Royal Canadian Mounted Police color guard carried the U.S. flag during the pregame national anthem ceremonies, the Marines carried the Canadian flag, this time right side up. The Canadians' graciousness was appreciated, and in the end they had the last laugh, as the Blue Jays took the Series in six games.

UMPIRES

Nobody has loved umpiring more than Tom Gorman, the universally respected arbiter who worked in the National League from 1951 through the 1976 season. The only reason Gorman quit umpiring when he did is that he had reached the league's mandatory retirement age of 55. Moreover, when Gorman died in August of 1986, he was buried, per his request, in his umpiring uniform with a ball-strike indicator in his hand. The count on the indicator was 3 and 2 . . . the same as the title of his autobiography, published in 1979.

There's an old adage, "No one ever paid his way into a ball game to watch the umpires," that's meant to caution umpires from getting an inflated sense of self-importance. The Upper Deck baseball card company has always known of this adage, but former National League umpire Joe West apparently never heard of it.

West threatened to sue Upper Deck for the "unauthorized use of his likeness" because a photo of him at work appeared on the *back* of card number 248 in Upper Deck's 1990 set. The fact that card number 248 is devoted to a player, Pirates outfielder Gary Redus, who is shown on the back of the card leaping back toward the bag as Cubs first baseman Mark

Grace awaits a pickoff throw (and umpire West looks on), meant nothing to the aggrieved arbiter.

Probably to avoid the nuisance and expense of a trial, Upper Deck settled out of court with West for an undisclosed amount of money. Upper Deck photo editors were presumably instructed from that point on to avoid in the future any photos that incidentally included umpires–as well as fans, ball girls, scoreboard operators, and ice-cream vendors.

Umpire Ron Luciano certainly never subscribed to the theory that umpires should strive to be unnoticed and anonymous. An ex–Syracuse University football player, Luciano was notorious for his flamboyant umpiring style— he would make his hand a pistol and "shoot" baserunners out—and after he retired he remained in the public spotlight. He was mediocre as a color commentator for ABC Sports, but Luciano later coauthored several humorous and highly successful baseball books.

Most people appreciated Luciano's attempts to add some levity to baseball during his umpiring career, but Baltimore Orioles manager Earl Weaver could hardly stand to be in the same ballpark with Ron, and once Weaver started complaining, Luciano usually felt the same way about him. The Luciano-Weaver feud dated back to the first meeting between the two in the low minor leagues. It was a four-game series, and Luciano threw Weaver out of the first game in the third inning, tossed him from the second game in the second inning, ejected him from the third game in the first inning, and threw him out of the series finale before the game even started. Luciano said, "Our relationship went downhill from there."

Weaver's animus for Luciano later caused him sometimes to go to ridiculous extremes. One time Luciano was behind the plate for a game between the Orioles and the Oakland A's when Oakland's third baseman, Sal Bando, in the midst of a horrendous slump, came to bat. As Bando dug in, he said, "Ron, what am I doing wrong?"

Luciano said, "I have no idea, Sal, but I know that you're standing farther away from the plate than you used to."

The next night Bando hit a 500-foot home run against the Orioles. As he rounded third, the exultant Bando cried, "Ron, that was it!" Luciano gave Bando a big smile and shook his hand.

After the game an infuriated Weaver wrote a letter to the American League president complaining that Luciano was now coaching the players on opposing teams on how to beat him.

After putting in a long and difficult minor league apprenticeship, Emmett Ashford became the first black umpire in the majors. Ashford was able to successfully break baseball's second color barrier because he went about the job of umpiring with intelligence, flair, and a sense of humor. Emmett showed he could handle anybody, even Leo Durocher, the nastiest umpire-baiter in the history of baseball.

Durocher's Chicago Cubs were in the field during a spring training game when Ashford was working behind the plate. A batter on the opposing team took a half-swing, and Ashford ruled the pitch a ball. Durocher charged from the dugout toward Ashford, screaming, "What was it? What was it?"

On disputed check swings, the home-plate umpire usually consults with the first- or third-base umpire, because the latter presumably has a better view of the play. Thus, Ashford took off his mask and pointed toward the first-base ump, who of course was white. Without hesitation, the first-base umpire signaled "safe," indicating that the batter had not swung the bat across the plate.

Durocher ran down to first to argue but was completely ignored. He then ran back to home plate shouting, "It was a strike. It was a strike." Ashford allowed Durocher to carry on for a few moments more, but finally he jutted his face close to Durocher's and said magisterially, "Leo, it was not a strike . . . and you've got it in black and white."

When the umpiring decisions are going against them, ballplayers sometimes complain that they are playing "nine against thirteen." The Chicago Cubs surely wondered if they were about to face such a situation in Cincinnati on April 25, 1990, when the umpiring crew of Terry Tata, Jerry Crawford, Bill Hohn, and Ed Rapuano took the field dressed in Cincinnati Reds windbreakers and gray road uniforms.

All appearances to the contrary, the umps had not renounced their cherished impartiality; their luggage was simply late in arriving from Houston, and they had had to improvise with help from the Reds' equipment manager, Bernie Stowe. Fortunately, Tata and his colleagues were all reasonably slim in build. If Eric Gregg and other umpires as massive as he had been involved, there's no way Stowe would have been able to outfit them.

The legend of how umpiring signals for balls and strikes came about is well known. Because he was deaf, 19th-century outfielder William Ellsworth "Dummy" Hoy could not hear the umpire's ball-strike calls. His teammates on the Cincinnati Red Stockings began indicating the calls to Hoy via hand signals from the dugout, and it wasn't long before the umpires followed suit, first with Hoy and then as standard practice with all batters.

Not so well known is the story about why former umpire Augie Donatelli adopted his unusual umpiring stance behind home plate. Donatelli was working the plate during a 1961 game in Cincinnati, and the crouching he did in the umpire's normal stance was sending his hemorrhoids into an uproar on every pitch. Between innings Donatelli rested on one knee to relieve the pain, and he realized that he might be able to umpire from that position. Sure enough, Donatelli could see the plate fine and found that the stance even gave him a better view of the low outside pitch. The only trouble was that he had a little trouble keeping his balance on one knee. To steady himself he rested a hand on the back of Cincinnati catcher Jerry Zimmerman. Finding the umpire's touch a bit distracting, Zimmerman asked, "Hey, Augie, is it legal for the umpire to touch a player?"

"It is now," snapped Donatelli, who was not about to let the rule book interfere with his newfound comfort.

Ken Kaiser tells a story that proves that sometimes an umpire's greatest asset is his ability to defuse an argument before it gets started.

"I was umpiring a Tigers game one day," says Kaiser, "when Ralph Houk was the Detroit manager. The Tigers were in the field, and on a close play at first I called the runner safe. Houk came out and said, 'What happened?'

"I pointed over at the Tigers' first baseman and said, 'He tagged the base with the wrong foot.'

"Houk nodded his head and walked halfway back to the dugout before he stopped and said, 'Wait a minute, he can tag the base with either foot!'"

When it comes to professional baseball, Cincinnati is known as the "City of Firsts"; one first Cincinnati could have done without was the death of an umpire on the diamond during a game.

Home-plate umpire John McSherry died of "sudden cardiac arrest" (a heart attack) only seven pitches into the game between the Reds and the Montreal Expos at Riverfront Stadium on Monday, April 1, 1996. It seemed like the cruelest of April Fools' jokes, and it ruined Opening Day, which is normally celebrated as the most exuberant of public holidays in Cincinnati.

McSherry, a huge man with a history of weight-related health problems, knew that he had a serious heart condition, an irregular heartbeat. He had been urged to skip his assignment on Opening Day to see a doctor, but he refused and intended to make that visit the following day, on Tuesday, when the Reds and Expos were to have enjoyed an off-day.

Expos coach Jim Tracy noticed that McSherry slurred his words during the pregame exchange of lineup cards but thought nothing of it. The first pitch was another warning sign that nobody recognized. Reds starting pitcher Pete Schourek delivered his first pitch to Expos second baseman Mark Grudzielanek right down the middle, but McSherry made no call whatsoever. The Reds' official scorers assumed this meant McSherry thought the pitch was a ball and recorded it as such on the stadium scoreboard.

McSherry recovered and began to call balls and strikes as normal. Everything seemed fine until, after another no-call pitch to Rondell White, he called time-out, gestured toward second-base umpire Steve Ripley, and then turned around and began walking off the field toward an exit behind home plate. Just before he reached the exit, McSherry collapsed and fell prostrate, facedown, still wearing his mask and chest protector. Reds trainers and team physicians, Montreal trainers, and at least three other doctors attending the game who vaulted from the stands arrived within seconds to administer to the fallen umpire. As stunned silence reigned throughout the ballpark, they worked frantically on McSherry for a quarter of an hour, but all attempts to revive him were unsuccessful.

McSherry was removed from the field on a stretcher, and 15 minutes later he was taken by ambulance to University Hospital. Umpire Tom Hallion, who had been weeping considerably, rode along in the ambulance.

At first, the two remaining umpires, Ripley and Jerry Crawford, intended (out of a sense of duty) to continue the game after a half-hour warm-up period. But it quickly became obvious that the players on both teams were too upset to concentrate on baseball and felt, moreover, that the proper thing to do would be to postpone the game, out of respect for the universally liked and respected McSherry. Reds shortstop Barry Larkin put the players' feelings into words most eloquently when he told Reds manager Ray Knight, "Ray, I've had a lot of deaths in my family. In good conscience, out of respect for life, I can't go out there."

Some people, including Reds owner Marge Schott, disagreed with the decision to postpone the game, but the majority clearly felt it was appropriate to make a statement affirming the priority of respect for life over the playing of a game. The following day saw a rare, if not another unique, event in baseball history. As the umpires walked onto the field prior to the start of the makeup game, Cincinnati fans showered them with a standing ovation that expressed sympathy, understanding, and appreciation.

On the same day, it was announced that flags at major league ballparks would fly at half-mast for the rest of the week and that National League umpires would wear black armbands on their uniform shirts the rest of the season. Testimonials to McSherry and to his love of baseball and his profession came from many, but it was former major league pitcher and legendary Reds radio announcer Joe Nuxhall who uttered the most consoling words possible: "You see a lot of things in baseball, but you'd like not to be there for something like this. I do know if you could wake John up, he'd tell you that if he had to go, there couldn't have been a better place than on the ballfield."

BOB VEALE

John Curtis pitched in the major leagues for 15 years for five different teams. He didn't last that long without learning a few things about pitching, including the fact that "it takes more than a good arm to pitch effectively in the big leagues." Pitchers will do whatever it takes to get a crucial out in a ball game, and sometimes that even means acting a little crazy.

"When I was with the Cardinals," says Curtis, "Lou Brock told me a story about the time he thinks he may have been psyched out by Bob Veale of the Pittsburgh Pirates. Lou is up against Veale in the ninth inning at Forbes Field with the tying run on second base. Now, Bob Veale was a great big left-hander who wore glasses and threw about 100 mph. I mean, Veale could bring it. A second thing about Veale was that he sweated profusely whenever he pitched. He was famous for it. And since this was a very hot summer night, the sweat was just dripping off him.

"The way Brock tells the story, Veale's glasses are continually fogging up so bad he can't see. After every pitch Veale stomps off the back of the mound, pulls off his cap, wipes his brow, and tries to dry off his glasses.

"Well, after the count goes to 2–2, Veale gets so irritated at the fact that his glasses keep fogging up that he rips them off his face and throws them over toward the third-base dugout. The third baseman, Maury Wills, picks the glasses up and takes them over to the mound. Wills tries to get Veale to take his glasses, but Veale won't even look at them. Veale climbs back on the rubber and gets ready to pitch, still sweating like a sumo wrestler in a sauna, except that now he's also squinting terribly.

"Veale winds up and fires a fastball, and the pitch comes in around 100 mph but a foot over Brock's head.

"Well, Brock is ready to duck the next pitch too. The last thing he's thinking about now is hitting the ball, so Veale throws the 3–2 pitch right down the middle for strike three.

"Lou said, 'To this day, I don't know if Veale set me up or not. At the time I really didn't care. I was just glad to get out of the batter's box alive.'"

LARRY WALKER

Losing track of the number of outs is one of the dumbest things a ballplayer can do. So is giving away a ball in play as a souvenir. On April 24, 1994, in a game at Dodger Stadium, Montreal Expos outfielder Larry Walker pulled both bonehead stunts on one play.

With one out and a man on first, Dodgers catcher Mike Piazza lifted a fly ball down the right-field line. Walker made the catch in foul ground and, thinking he'd just corralled the third out of the inning, walked over to the box seats, handed the ball to a boy sitting in the first row, and headed for the dugout. A few seconds later Walker woke up in time to see Los Angeles shortstop Jose Offerman, who had tagged up at first, rounding second and heading for third. Walker ran back to the scene of the crime, retrieved the ball from the boy, who handed it over willingly, and fired it back into the infield in time to keep Offerman from scoring. Offerman scored anyway when Tim Wallach hit a two-run homer, but at least Offerman's run was not a direct result of Walker's blunder.

When the Expos headed back onto the field for the bottom of the fourth, Walker took a new ball with him and presented it to the boy who had been so cooperative the inning before. Walker's thoughtfulness netted him a standing ovation from the hometown crowd and warm receptions every time he came to bat during the rest of the game. Despite the unaccustomed assistance and appreciation of the opposing fans, Walker and the Expos lost the game 7–1.

221

EARL WEAVER

In 17 seasons as the manager of the Baltimore Orioles, Earl Weaver won 1,480 games, six division titles, four American League pennants, and one World Championship. A cerebral manager, Weaver kept and made extensive use of records about opponents' tendencies, and he ran a ball game as if it were a chess match.

When Weaver was inducted into the Hall of Fame, he thanked everyone he could think of, including the umpires. "They must have made over a million calls while I was managing," he said, "and except for the 91 times I disagreed with them, they got every single one of those calls right."

If you're not among those attuned to the particulars of Weaver's career, the 91 times he "disagreed with the umpires" refers to the number of occasions on which he was ejected from games for arguing disagreeably with the umps, a major league record.

Ken Singleton, the former Orioles outfielder who now works as a broadcaster for the Montreal Expos, remembers one year when he got off to a bad start, batting only about .125 after the first month of the season.

"Earl called me into his office for a little chat. 'Kenny, you're not hitting as well as you usually do,' he said. 'Is something wrong?'

" 'No, nothing's wrong,' I said.

" 'Are you sick?' he asked.

" 'No.'

" 'Are you tired?' he asked.

" 'No.'

" 'Well, I'm sick and tired of you not hitting!' he said."

Sportswriter and author Joe Durso tells a whimsical story about Weaver and Davey Johnson, who, as Weaver's second baseman for seven years, learned so much that he became a fine major league manager in his own right.

According to Durso, "Johnson wasn't content just to play second base. He was also a student of math and spent many of his free evenings at the Johns Hopkins University working on a project he called 'The Optimization of the Baltimore Orioles Lineup.' His project involved putting Orioles players into the computer to see what would happen if crazy things were done to their lineup, like having Frank Robinson lead off. When Johnson finished the project, he took a typed summary of it to Weaver. A few days later a sportswriter asked Johnson what Weaver thought about his study. 'Earl threw it in the wastebasket,' Johnson said dejectedly. The sportswriter sympathized with Johnson but mentally agreed with Weaver's reaction, because in his opinion Baltimore's success under Weaver proved that Earl had *already* optimized the Orioles' lineup."

When Weaver first heard this story his comment was: "The reason I threw Johnson's report in the garbage is that all his lineups had him batting cleanup."

Currently an advance scout for the Colorado Rockies, former catcher Rick Dempsey burns brightest in the minds of baseball fans as the MVP of the 1983 World Series. Rick's home run and four doubles for a .385 batting average led Baltimore to a victory in five games over the Philadelphia Phillies. As Dempsey spent the prime of his 21-year major league career with the Orioles from 1976 through 1986, he got to know Weaver and his peccadilloes all too well.

"Whenever I'd make a mistake, Earl would threaten to take me out of the game," says Dempsey. "He'd say things like, 'If that guy hits another fastball, you're out of the game.' After a while, I learned to ignore him.

"One night we were playing the Indians, and we were batting. Larry Harlow was on second, and I was on first. A pitch got away from the Indians' catcher, and Larry and I started running. I got all the way to second, but for some reason Larry stopped halfway between second and third and then ran back to second. We were both standing there at second, so I told Larry, 'You stay here, I'll go back to first.' Well, I got thrown out trying to get back to first, and Earl got mad at me. 'You're out of the game, Dempsey,' he shouted.

"I ignored him as usual, put my gear on, and went out to warm up our pitcher. Earl came out to home plate, really steamed, criticizing me the whole time. He showed me the lineup card and pointed to the number nine spot in the batting order. 'Whose name is that?' he asked.

"'Mine, Earl,' I said.

"He held the card up, right in my face, and scribbled all over my name, completely blacked it out. 'You're out of the game! Get off the field!' he shouted.

"I still ignored him, so then Earl started screaming that he was going to forfeit the game if I didn't leave the field. He was threatening to have his own team forfeit; that's how mad he was.

"Frank Robinson, one of Earl's coaches at that time, came over and said, 'Rick, I think he means it this time. You'd better leave.'

"With Earl still screaming at me, I walked off the field. Now I was mad. When I got into the dugout, I started taking off my stuff and throwing it, piece by piece, at Earl. He'd pick it up and throw it right back at me. This went on for five minutes: my shin guards, chest protector, cap, cup, mask . . . flying back and forth in the dugout, Earl and me yelling at each other. Everybody in the whole stadium stopped what they were doing and watched. Finally, Frank Robinson grabbed me in a bear hug, and somebody else grabbed Earl, or the catcher's equipment would still be flying.

"I went into the clubhouse to cool off and take a shower, but Earl followed me, still cussing and screaming. He even followed me into the shower room, so I turned the shower on him, completely soaking him. That finally shut him up."

ED WHITSON

You can understand if ex-pitcher Ed Whitson never wants to step foot inside New York City again. That's because Yankees fans booed him out of town in 1986, after first booing him out of the starting rotation for home games. Here's how this bizarre circumstance came about.

Whitson's Big Apple nightmare began in 1985 when he signed a $4.4 million free-agent contract with the Yankees. Expectations among New York's demanding fans were high, and when Whitson got off to a 1–6 start, Yankees fans began booing him unmercifully. Worse, a few lunatics periodically threatened harm to him and to his family. Over the winter the Yankees tried to trade Whitson, as the good old country boy from Johnson City, Tennessee, had requested, but the big contract proved to be a stumbling block, and Ed was back with the Yankees when the 1986 season opened.

On April 9, Whitson started in Yankee Stadium against the Kansas City Royals. Clearly feeling an undue amount of pressure before he took the mound, Whitson said, "To me, this is bigger than a World Series game." It was an ominous reference, as Whitson had started the second game of the 1984 World Series for the San Diego Padres but lasted only two-thirds of an inning, surrendering five hits and three runs. Against the Royals, Whitson was relieved after two and two-thirds innings; the dreaded booing began as soon as he gave up a single to the first batter of the game, Lonnie Smith. Whitson was so obviously rattled that the Yankees subsequently announced the previously unheard-of policy of having him start only road games for an indefinite period. "This gives him a chance to relax, get some things under his belt and build up his confidence," said Yankees manager Lou Piniella. It also gave the media a chance to mock both the pitcher and the Yankees' ploy.

Whitson was scratched from his next scheduled start at home on April 21, but he did pitch in Yankee Stadium in relief on April 27 and 29. His second start of the season at home did not come until June 8, when he lasted but two-thirds of an inning against the Baltimore Orioles. It was his last start wearing Yankee pinstripes. His final five appearances as a Yankee came in relief, but Whitson's fate in New York had been sealed long before. On July 9 he escaped from New York in a trade that sent him back to San Diego for another pitcher, Tim Stoddard. Free of the New York boo birds, Whitson steadily improved his record for the Padres in the next three seasons, pitching on the road and at home as his position in the starting rotation dictated.

ANTHONY YOUNG

Nobody likes to lose, but losing really got old for Young; that is, New York Mets pitcher Anthony Young, whose personal consecutive-game losing streak over the 1992 and '93 seasons reached a staggering 27! Young's amazing streak shattered the previous record of 23 consecutive losses strung together by Boston Braves pitcher Cliff Curtis over the 1910 and 1911 seasons.

The first loss of Young's streak came on May 6, 1992, at Cincinnati. Young lost his next 12 decisions of 1992 and then his first 14 decisions of 1993 before finally copping a win on July 28, 1993, in New York against the expansion Florida Marlins.

During the streak Young made a total of 74 appearances and went 0–14 as a starter, 0–13 as a reliever (he was 0–16 at home, 0–11 on the road). Why did the Mets keep sending Young out to the mound? Well, for one thing, they didn't have anybody better; the once-mighty Mets, after all, had sunk to the bottom of the major leagues. After Young's streak-ending victory on the 28th of July, the Mets were lodged securely in the basement of the National League Eastern Division, a full seven games behind the sixth-place Marlins. For another thing, Young's pitching during the streak wasn't all bad, as he recorded 15 saves to go along with the 27 losses.

Young's streak was not a trip to Disneyland, but at least it ended in dramatic fashion. Young came on to pitch the ninth in relief of starter Bret Saberhagen with the score tied 2–2. It looked like defeat number 28 when the Marlins took the lead by plating an unearned run off Young, but the Mets won the game in the bottom of the inning, scoring two runs off Marlins ace reliever Bryan Harvey.

Not only did the Mets and their fans perform an imitation of a World Series celebration, but also fans around the league rejoiced when news of Young's victory was flashed on their teams' scoreboards. After the game a relieved and suddenly optimistic Young said, "I knew it couldn't go on like that forever. Now I hope to get 27 wins in a row."

INDEX